by

Simon Worsfold

Illustrated by Graham Robson

Public Eye Publications

A Public Eye Publications Book

www.thegreatestintheworld.com

Illustrations:
Graham Robson, 'Drawing the Line'
info@dtline.co.uk

Cover design:
pentacorbig:
book & information graphic design
www.pentacorbig.co.uk

Layout design:
Bloomfield Ltd.

Copy editor:
Bronwyn Robertson
www.theartsva.com

Series creator / editor:
Steve Brookes

This first edition published in 2007 by
Public Eye Publications, PO Box 3182,
Stratford-upon-Avon, Warwickshire CV37 7XW

Text and Illustrations Copyright © 2007 - Public Eye Publications

'The Greatest in the World' Copyright © 2004 - Anne Brookes

A CIP catalogue record for this book is available from the British Library
ISBN 9781-905151-16-5

Printed and bound by Biddles Books Limited, King's Lynn, Norfolk PE30 4LS

This book is dedicated to my loving wife and family.
Also to all the people I've met on my travels who have shown
me what a wonderful world we have and how important it is we
save it for the future.

Contents

A Few Words from Simon...

In the first tourism job I had, running a sunny campsite on the shores of Lake Garda in Northern Italy, the first thing my boss told me was that people on holiday always forget to pack their brain. This was a bit harsh, I thought, knowing that campers were about the most resourceful holidaymakers going and besides, I wouldn't be getting to know any of them that well.

So I discarded his advice as the words of a man jaded by years of waiting on other people when really. all he wanted was for other people to wait on him. But then, to my alarm, as we crept towards peak season, I actually began to see what he meant.

As the empty sites filled up, I found myself surrounded by people from all over Western Europe – Holland, Germany, Italy, Austria and Britain – who all seemed to need more hand-holding than most children on their first day at school. They would ask questions like: "Do you wash our clothes for us here?" and even "Is it safe to swim in the lake? I'm worried about sea snakes."

I was dumbfounded. Here was a group of ordinary, intelligent adults incapable of figuring out the simplest things for themselves. People old enough to be my parents who were utterly reliant on me.

And then it hit me. These people didn't forget to pack their brains at all. They had done it on purpose! Switching off was all part of their luxury of being on holiday. And in a sense, at the end of the day, it is what you pay for. Because when you've worked so hard to earn it, your time off is sacred, and nothing gets in the way of a good holiday. Not even the old noggin!

But it also made me realise, on my own travels years later, that you mustn't let the pleasure you get from disengaging cause you, at best, to miss out on something or, at worst, leave you at risk. Hence the 'Greatest Travel Tips in the World'. Not a cultural crash course or in depth city guide, just a handy little book for any trip you dare to plan. Whether you're visiting the relatives in Richmond or packing off to the cloud forests of Costa Rica, once you've read this book you can consider your brain packed.

Happy travelling!

The Greatest Travel Tips in the World

Chapter 1 – Booking Your Holiday

Enjoy it!

The first rule of travel is: enjoy it. As many wise people have said "happiness is a journey, not a destination", so whether you're preparing for the big trip or already en route, sit back and soak it up. Seeing the world is a privilege and by appreciating it from the moment you book, you'll make more of the holiday itself.

A change is as good as a rest

When life gets hectic, holidays are the most important weeks of the year, which means you've got to make the most of them. The best route to relaxation is to get as far away from your daily routine as possible so you can completely unwind. If you go on holiday to do the same things you do at home, you're not going to come back feeling any more refreshed!

What do you want?

Before you book, think about what you want to get out of your holiday. Are you looking for relaxation? Excitement? To get fit? To meet someone? The answer will help you choose the right kind of break. If you're travelling in a group, it is even more important to find out what everyone wants beforehand so you can all have a good time.

Take the temperature

Like an Aussie cooking a 'barbie' on the beach in the middle of December, remember it's not always cold at Christmas! If you're expecting a holiday of cool fresh air you don't want to arrive in the middle of a heat wave (or vice versa), so use a world weather guide like Fodor's, *www.worldclimate.com* or *www.worldweather.org* to make sure you get the weather you booked.

Party animal

We all hate to miss a good party, but imagine starting your holiday to discover you missed the country's biggest festival only a few days before. To find out what's going on where you're going to be, use *www.earthcalendar.net* or *www.whatsonwhen.com* to plan your next trip. What is Rio without the carnival, after all?

Sporting journeys

International sports events like the football World Cup always bring out the best in the host country and this makes it a fantastic time to visit, even if you don't have tickets for the games. You'll need to book ahead but there are many specialist tour operators out there providing itineraries for everything from 'Barmy Army' cricket tours to the traditional 'Naadam' Olympics in Mongolia.

13

Get online

Even if you end up booking in person with a travel agent, always check out a number of deals online first to find the best price. That way you'll know as soon as you've got a good deal and, if you haven't, just tell the travel agent how much you've been quoted and see if they will match the price. Most will.

Package or DIY?

The internet hasn't brought an end to the package holiday but it has given us a lot more flexibility. If you 'do it yourself' by booking your flights and accommodation separately, it's a good idea to book two different hotels for the first night and cancel one as soon as you know you've got a good room. Hotels have been known to give away booked rooms to people without reservations just to be sure they get the business, and a cancellation fee is always better than being left on the street on the first night of your holiday.

Bargain basement

There are some great deals out there and with more people flying than ever before, the non-environmentalists among us would say we've been in a 'golden age' of cheap airline travel recently. How long this continues remains to be seen, but for now remember, the bigger the discount the greater the restrictions, so don't expect a refund if you have to cancel, and do expect to be getting up very early for the flight.

Save paper, time and money

Many tour operators now make their brochures available online. This not only saves paper and time, but could even help to hold down the price of your holiday. Travel brochures may be free to you, but they are expensive to print and at the end of the day, that's all factored into the cost of your holiday. To save you having to search through hundreds of websites for the right brochure, go straight to *www.brochurebank.co.uk*.

Be inspired

There are many good travel magazines and websites with inspiration for your next trip, but for more up front reviews about the places you're thinking of visiting use internet forums like Lonely Planet's 'Thorn Tree' (*www.lonelyplanet. co.uk*) or Holiday Watchdog (*www.holidaywatchdog.com*) to read reviews written by people who haven't been paid to go there.

Stuck for ideas?

If you're not a regular newspaper or travel magazine reader, another good place for holiday ideas is a travel show. They are attended by hundreds of tour operators offering just about every type of holiday imaginable. Many also run special offers just for the show so you might be able to bag a bargain to boot.

A photo never lies

To find out if the 'luxury beachfront hotel' advertised in your holiday brochure is really what it says it is, use *www.tripadvisor.com*. It has photos of hotel rooms all over the world taken by fellow travellers to show what they are really like. Definitely worth a look to see if the 'idyllic' place you're about to book is included.

Confirm your flight

With every flight, but especially when buying online, always call the airline a day or two before you fly to confirm your booking has gone through and that they are expecting you. It's also worth checking that you have a seat allocation because if you don't and your flight is overbooked, you could be the one left on the tarmac.

Arriving safely

If you're travelling alone or with young children, try to avoid booking a flight that arrives in the middle of the night because it will leave you tired and more vulnerable during the first few hours in the country. If you can't avoid arriving in the middle of the night, arrange for a representative from your hotel to come and meet you at the airport.

Top Ten Far Out Holidays

1. Cycling through the tropical jungles of Guatemala and Honduras.
2. Staying in an ice hotel above the Arctic Circle in Sweden.
3. Riding the Trans-Mongolian Railway from Moscow to Beijing.
4. Sleeping underground in a cave hotel in Spain.
5. Learning to cook on a residential course in Thailand.
6. Scuba diving in the Cayman Islands.
7. Sailing through the Arctic on an ice breaker cruise ship.
8. Getting high in the Brazilian Amazon in a treetop hotel.
9. Keeping dry in the deep in an underwater hotel in Florida.
10. Aligning your chakras on a yogic retreat in India.

Chapter 2 – Getting Ready to Go

Do your research

Knowing about your destination helps you choose the right holiday and keeps you safe when you get there. Travel Guides like Footprint and Lonely Planet are a great starting point, but to really get inside a country ask your local bookstore for books written by people who actually live there. They will give a lot more insight.

Get a second opinion

As well as reading up on what to do at your destination, it's also worth reading up on what not to do. For up-to-date safety advice, check a number of official sources like the British Foreign and Commonwealth Office website (see *www.fco.gov.uk* and go to the 'travel advice by country' section) and the U.S. Department of State (see *www.state.gov* and go to the 'travel warnings' section). They will give you the updates that didn't make it into the last edition of your travel guide.

Ditch the travel guide

Travel guides are best for choosing destinations, not hotels, so if you buy one make sure you read it before you fly. Try not to rely on it too much when you arrive either, as prices may be 10-20% higher than quoted and many of the hotels listed will be crowded with all the people who bought the same book! The best way to beat the crowds is to be a little adventurous and be open to recommendations from locals and tourists alike.

Pocket book

To get the best out of your travel guide, make notes on all the places you'd most like to visit before you go and take these with you instead of the entire book. That way, you can fit all the information you need into your pocket and, now that you're no longer tied to your travel 'bible', you're free to explore all the lesser known places it didn't tell you about.

Local know-how

Do you know what all tourist information has in common? It always paints a good picture of a place, never a bad one. This is great for selling holidays, but not so great at telling you about any potential risks of travelling there. The best sources of honest and up-to-date information are local newspapers. And thanks to the globalisation of English, most countries now have editions you can read. It's worth buying a copy as soon as you arrive.

Travel light, travel far

This is the best piece of travel advice going. The heavier your bag is, the more hassle you're going to have carrying it. Before you leave home try walking a mile with your bag fully packed, then decide if you've packed enough stuff. As a rule of thumb, the longer you're away, the less you should take because you'll be washing your clothes regularly and you'll have more opportunities to buy souvenirs.

How to pack less

The key to packing less is to take a washing line and travel wash. How many times have you come home with unused clothes because you've just worn your favourite outfits night after night? When you can wash (and dry) your clothes on holiday, you get to wear your best gear whenever you want to and you don't have to pack as much in the first place.

Mix and match

Efficient packing is all about mixing and matching your clothes. If all your tops match all your bottoms, you'll have less to carry and more outfits to wear. Try to avoid denim though as it's heavy and takes ages to dry if it gets wet.

What to take?

If you're stuck for ideas about what to take with you on holiday, there's a very handy website called the Universal Packing List (see *http://upl.codeq.info*) which suggests essential items for different trips depending on who's going where and when. It's a good idea to keep a note of what you've packed so you can check everything off the list when you leave the hotel and be certain you've left nothing behind.

Take a smaller bag

If you are a habitual over-packer who comes home from every holiday with half a suitcase of clothes you never wore, think about taking a smaller bag on your next trip. It will force you to pack less and give your back and shoulders a break.

Roll don't fold

When you're packing, try to roll soft cotton items like t-shirts and jeans instead of folding them. This not only reduces creasing but, in rounded luggage like backpacks and duffel bags, also saves space.

Bringing souvenirs home

When you travel it's worth packing an empty, lightweight bag just in case you go souvenir crazy and can't fit them all into your suitcase for the journey home. If you have a hard suitcase, you can use that to pack all the breakables padded by your clean clothes, and the soft bag for all your dirty washing.

To wheel or not to wheel?

Wheelie bags have become a bit of a hit in recent years and they're great on the smooth floors of an airport but can be a nightmare out on the roads. Dragging a bag with wheels around a city while it does a wrist-breaking 'R2D2 wobble' is a real pain. If you're going to be walking any distance, use a travel bag instead (see next tip). They're much easier to carry.

Compartmentalise

This is essential if you're moving about from place to place several times on your holiday. If you need your favourite shirt you don't want to have to unpack everything to get it, use stuff sacks (drawstring bags used for camping) or custom made packing cubes (available from most camping/travel stores) to separate your clothes into different compartments. They will save you a lot of hassle.

Take a day-pack

No holiday is complete without a day trip to see the sights, and it's really useful to have a small backpack with you for the camera and a few snacks. The best incorporate water bladders (made by companies like Platypus and Camelbak) so you can drink on the go.

Backpack or travel bag?

Purists will stand by their dual strap backpacks as the only way to go, but the more leisurely tourists among us will probably get more use out of a 'travel bag'. They combine the best aspects of a suitcase and backpack all in one – with both single and dual shoulder straps that smartly unzip from a panel on the back of the bag. This means you can hike with the best of them and still walk into a decent hotel without feeling like a backpacker. The other bonus is that you can check a travel bag into the hold of a plane without the straps getting damaged in transit.

Packing your valuables

Avoid packing valuables in your checked bags as they will be away from you for a long time on your journey, and might not be handled as carefully as you would like. It is best to keep your valuables on you at all times. If your luggage has outer pockets, never put anything delicate in them as it's unlikely to survive the journey.

Take miniatures

If you're only going away for a week or two, there's no need for family size bottles of shampoo. Instead, buy mini dispensers from your local chemist and fill them up from home with enough to last the trip. You can also get travel size toothpaste and even hairspray.

You scratch mine and I'll scratch yours

If you've got the sun cream, let your travel buddy take the after sun. You won't have as much to carry and there'll be no excuse for not getting a back rub every time you're in the sun!

Buy it there

If you didn't pack it – don't panic; just buy it when you get there! In most places things are cheaper than they are at home and will make a good souvenir. Note that this doesn't apply to sun cream or camera accessories as they're not always readily available and, where they are, can be pricey; so make sure you've got the right supplies.

Money talks

People say English is the global language but really it's numbers. '1, 2, 3' goes a lot further than 'one, two, three' so always pack a small calculator to help you through your price negotiations. You will always know how much you're being asked to pay and how much you're paying.

Holiday reading

A good book is essential on holiday but the last thing you want on the beach is a story about being eaten by sharks! The best holiday books reflect positively on the place you're visiting: like a novel set in a similar location or non-fiction that gives insight into the local way of life. Ask your bookstore for recommendations.

Keep it dry

Most luggage isn't waterproof and it is a nightmare to arrive at your hotel wearing two-day-old clothes to find everything soaking wet. Before you pack, line your luggage with a heavy duty bin liner or, if you have a backpack, buy a custom made waterproof cover from your local camping store.

Hands free

A head torch is one of the handiest items you can pack. It always shines where you need it and keeps your hands free at the same time: ideal for reading, finding your way back from the beach late at night, and packing for your return flight with the birds first thing in the morning. You can get them in most camping stores but the best deals are online.

Take a plug

Don't expect every hotel to supply one. If you can't wash or shave properly because the last tenant took the sink plug, it's the pits, especially after a long flight. Universal plugs are sold at most airports but you can always make your own by cutting a squash ball in half or, if you're travelling light, by buying a lemon when you arrive, cutting it in half and placing it over the plughole.

Dirty washing

Always pack an empty bag to fill with dirty washing. Linen bags are lightweight, but not waterproof, while canvas bags are waterproof, but not lightweight; so the best option is to use a sealed, lightweight stuff sack (available from most camping stores) to hold damp items and keep the smell at bay.

Bag it

Resealable food bags are a traveller's best friend. You can use them to stop your toiletries leaking, and with a few extra tucked away you'll be amazed at what other uses they have, from keeping your passport dry to packing wet swimming trunks.

Download your sounds

If you haven't joined the music download revolution yet, you might want to before your next trip. There's no easier way to carry music with you. The players are light, hold loads of songs and will plug in almost anywhere. Two things to remember though: first, back-up all your music at home in case anything goes wrong, and second, don't flash it about the place as an MP3 player is very attractive to thieves.

Sarong

Another essential travel item - even for guys – is a sarong. It's great on the beach and doubles as a towel, scarf, pillow, table cloth, shower wrap, toilet cubicle, and even a mobile changing room. It's also paper thin, lightweight, and dries in an instant.

Travel towel

How many times have you had to pack a beach towel while it was still wet? Or forgotten to pack it because it was still drying? Combined with a sarong to wrap around yourself, a travel towel is a much better option as it's smaller, more absorbent and dries much faster.

Shoe bag

You can't underestimate the value of a good shoe bag. You don't want to pack dirty shoes next to clean clothes and a zippable bag to keep them in is a good investment for any holiday. For extra protection, double wrap your shoes in a plastic bag.

Top Ten Places to See Wild Swarms!

1. One hundred million red crabs -
   Christmas Island, Indian Ocean, Australia.

2. Two million wildebeest -
   Plains of Botswana, North Namibia, South Zimbabwe.

3. Two million jellyfish -
   Micronesian island of Palau.

4. Eighty thousand migrating storks -
   Ban Thasadet, Thailand.

5. Two million free-tailed bats -
   The caves of Gunung Mulu National Park, Borneo.

6. Thousands of caribou -
   Ivvavik National Park, Canadian Arctic.

7. Thousands of squeaking grunions -
   Beaches of southwestern California.

8. Millions of mayflies -
   Mississippi River, La Crosse, Wisconsin, US.

9. Millions of monarch butterflies -
   Angangueo, Mexico.

10. Thousands of turtles -
    Tamar Project, beaches of the Brazilian coastline.

Chapter 3 –
Looking After Your Documents

How old is your passport?

You don't just need a passport to leave a country; you need one to get back in as well. Before you fly, check that yours doesn't expire while you're away. As a rule of thumb, you should never travel with less than six months' validity because this is an entry requirement in many countries. Some countries now require machine-readable passports so be sure that yours is modern enough to get you where you want to go.

Do you take visa?

It's not just restaurants that take Visa, Customs Officials do too. Find out well in advance what travel permits you need to visit a country as visas are almost impossible to obtain at short notice. In your capital city, contact the embassy or consulate of the country you will be visiting, or see their website for information.

Applying for a visa

The ease of obtaining a visa will depend on where you want to go and why. Some countries simply issue them the moment you arrive, while others may require a personal letter of invitation. If you have to go to the country's embassy in your capital city to apply for a visa in advance, make sure you have all the right documents, identification and photographs with you because there's no flexibility if you forget something. Note that journalists and those on business trips usually require non-tourist visas.

Take your receipts

One of the great advantages of booking online is that you can save money by paying for your flight and accommodation separately. But this also means you'll have more confirmations to remember. They are usually sent by email so check your junk/spam mailbox as well as your inbox, then print them out and staple them together. Check that each printout is clear because many airlines now use machine-readable barcodes for check-in.

Security wallet

A security wallet is a pouch for your money and travel documents that can be worn around the neck, chest, waist or leg. They're not always as secure as the name suggests, but they are useful for keeping everything in one place. They come in various shapes and sizes but whichever one you choose, make sure you keep it out of sight at all times as they are a magnet for thieves.

Hand in your departure card

If you have to complete a card on the airplane or in customs when you arrive at your destination (e.g. when flying to America from Britian), make sure you hand in the 'departure' section when you finally leave the country. If you fly home with this card, it goes on record that you never left the country and thus overstayed your visit. This is fine until you fly back to that country, at which point you will be detained until the matter is cleared up.

Hiring a car?

If you want to drive away from your destination airport in a hire car, many countries require an International Driving Permit as well as your own. Your local driving agency will be able to tell you if you need one and where you can get it but even if it's not mandatory, it's a good idea to get one as they're printed in several languages and may help to smooth over any over-zealous officials you run into.

Wear and tear

If your passport becomes too worn or damaged you can have a lot of trouble in Customs and could even be refused entry. When you travel a lot it's worth investing in a durable cover to keep your passport neat and tidy. Some hotels give out complimentary branded passport covers to their guests, so to save a bit of cash, ask at the front desk next time you stay somewhere.

Email to the rescue

To be extra safe, scan a copy of all your important documents (your passport photo page, visa, driving licence, air tickets and credit and debit cards) into your computer and send the files as attachments to a web-based email account like *www.hotmail.com* or *www.gmail.com*. If you lose everything you can simply log on and print off what you need to get money and get home.

Did you know?

The word atlas has only been associated with geography since the late sixteenth century when Rumold Mercator used a drawing of Atlas the Titan holding a globe above his shoulders as the frontispiece to his book of world maps. What's even more interesting about this is that Greek mythology makes no mention of this feat whatsoever.

Photocopy everything

Always carry photocopies of your passport photo page, visa, driving licence, insurance documents, air tickets and credit or debit card when you travel, and keep them away from the originals in case you lose them. It's also a good idea to stash some cash (Sterling or U.S. Dollars) with the photocopies in case of an emergency.

Chapter 4 – Surviving the Airport

Safe parking

There's no way round it, parking at airports costs a fortune and you're better off getting a lift from a friend. If you have to drive, leave the car in an official car park as the cheaper, local alternatives have been known to 'use' or even 'lose' holidaymakers' cars while they're away. Wherever you leave it, make sure you park it yourself and take the keys with you.

Book in advance

Many airports have their own parking facilities that let you reserve a space in advance and might even give you a discount for doing so. It's well worth the trouble for the extra security and peace of mind; contact your local airport authority for information.

Getting through security

Tougher security means that check-in times are much longer than they used to be. On international flights, they can be up to three hours so make sure you leave plenty of time and check the road conditions beforehand. Wear socks as well as shoes because many airports will now scan passengers' shoes as well as their hand luggage. Finally, check with the airport or your airline for what you can and can't take with you, as fluctuating levels of security mean that restrictions can change without warning.

Fruit flies

Fruit is perfect plane food but be careful: many countries, like Chile and New Zealand, have strict quarantine controls that dole out hefty fines if you happen to walk through Customs carrying an illegal banana.

Go strapless

No matter what bag you have – suitcase, travelbag or backpack – always remove or secure the straps before you check it in so they don't get damaged in transit.

Unhappy birthday

If you're flying out to a celebration and have presents packed in your checked luggage, make sure they're not wrapped. If your bags are hand searched by security, they will unwrap them to check what's inside. Pack the paper, tape and ribbon separately.

Checking in

If you booked your tickets online, you might be able to save time by checking in your own luggage at the airport, so don't forget your security password or barcode if you were issued one. One of the questions you will be asked is whether you packed the bags yourself so if you're carrying a bag for a friend, be sure you pack it with them and know what's inside. It's strictly prohibited to carry unknown items.

45

Getting the right seat

Many airlines now offer online check-in and if this is available, you should make your reservation as early as possible to get a good seat. To find out which is the best seat, use *www.seatguru.com* where the seats on most commercial airplanes are rated according to comfort. Be aware that even when you 'reserve' a seat online, the final allocation is only done when you check-in at the airport so always confirm with a member of staff when you get there. As a rule it's 'first come, first served' so if you must have more legroom expect to arrive early for it.

Don't lose your bottle!

Tighter airport security can make it harder to transport duty free bottles of alcohol these days. When security is tightest, you may only be allowed to carry unopened 100ml bottles of liquid in your hand luggage (which must be placed in separate, clear bags as you go through security). This presents no problem on direct flights as you only hit duty free after security, but if you have a connecting flight, the only way you will be able to keep your booze is if you can put it into an item of checked luggage. If you can't do this, the security personnel will get an early Christmas present!

Weight limits

Weight limits vary enormously from airline to airline and from route to route, often depending on how much you paid for your ticket. As a guide, long-haul flights tend to allow one item of hand luggage weighing up to 10kg and a maximum three bags of checked luggage weighing up to 23kg each. It's important to check the limits before any flight but especially when security is heightened because allowances can change with little or no warning.

Tipping the scales

The maximum weight limit on some long-haul flights can be as much as 70kg of luggage. But don't forget that there are still individual limits for each bag and if just one is over the limit, you will be charged an excess fee – even if you have not exceeded the total weight allowance. Always check the restrictions before you fly, weigh your bags at home and pack an empty bag to fill up, just in case.

Budget airlines

One of the ways budget airlines keep their costs down is to restrict luggage allowances. This could be as little as 15kg per person (not per bag) for checked luggage and 5kg for hand luggage, and the charge for exceeding this is significant. This isn't necessarily a bad thing though, as you'll have no choice but to pack lighter bags that are easier to carry.

Size limits

Again, these vary depending on which airline you fly and the level of security at the time of travel but as a rule of thumb, the dimensions of any checked bag should not exceed 158cm (after you have added the height to the width to the depth), while the dimensions of your hand luggage should not exceed 115cm. In times of heightened security, however, hand luggage allowances could be as little as 96cm, so always check with your airline before you fly.

Hand luggage

Hand luggage falls into two camps. If you like to travel light, it's a good idea not to overfill your hand luggage to keep room for a book or bottle from the Duty Free shops. But if you pack a lot when you travel, your hand luggage is perfect for single items that are either heavy, valuable or delicate as they are less likely to be lost or damaged in transit.

Duty-free

Duty-free goods in the airport are always cheaper than they are in the shops but they are often more expensive at your departure airport than they are at your destination airport – especially when flying from the U.K. The cheapest place to buy cigarettes is Africa and the Middle East, for electrical goods it's the Far East, while for wine and beer, continental European countries are a good bet. For a definitive guide of where to get the best value see *www. dutyfreeshoppingindex.com*, which compares duty-free prices between airports worldwide.

Prohibited items

This doesn't just cover drugs and guns but even innocuous items like nail clippers and cigarette lighters. Even bottles of mineral water can be banned when security is tightest so check with your airline before you fly to see what's in force. Whenever flying to a camping holiday, make sure you can buy the canisters for your gas stove at your destination before packing, because no airline will accept them on the plane.

50

Can't have creases?

If you're flying to a wedding or an important business meeting and you don't want to crease your suit or dress, keep it covered on the hanger and carry it onto the plane as an additional item of hand luggage (most airlines will let you carry a small bag as well). When you board, ask the flight attendant if they will hang it on the coat rail in first class. But don't forget to collect it!

Baggage receipts

These are the little barcodes attached to your boarding pass that match the flight labels on your checked bags. Don't lose them! If your bags go missing, you will need the receipts to get them back. If your bags are lost and you're left without clothes for more than a day, ask the airline to pay for replacements.

Dealing with delays

Delays are an inevitable hazard of flying that no one enjoys – especially on short breaks. To make sure it doesn't ruin your holiday, find out your new arrival time and get the airline to check that you can still reach your final destination safely at that time of day. If there's any chance you'll be left stranded, ask your airline to help you make alternative arrangements.

Stranded at the airport

If your flight is heavily delayed or even cancelled, your airline has a responsibility to look after you while you wait. In the U.K., for a two-hour delay they should supply a drink, a snack and two phone calls, for example. If you're delayed overnight, they should arrange dinner and accommodation for you – so make sure you don't pay for it yourself.

Short transfers

If you have a short transfer between international flights, don't panic – the plane shouldn't leave without you. All airports have a specified 'minimum connection time' and if your transfer is below this limit, there will be a contingency that allows you to be fast-tracked through to your connecting flight. If you are in any doubt, check with airline officials during check-in and again before you leave the plane to ensure you can be accommodated.

Airport navigation

Remember, especially with a family, that your holiday begins as soon as you enter the departure hall so be determined to make the whole experience an enjoyable one. This can be a cumbersome task but, with a little preparation, it needn't be. First, if you can, check in online before you leave home and leave plenty of time to get to the airport. Let the kids carry their own backpacks with music, books, toys or games but keep all the tickets and passports together in a single wallet for safety. As soon as you're through security, find a base and make sure everyone's occupied.

Did you know?

Japan's Kitakyushu Airport was built on a man-made island three kilometres off-shore in the Seto Sea.

Chapter 5 - Travelling with Ease

Flying

Some people love flying, other people hate it, but we all want it to go smoothly. Here's how. First, wear comfortable clothes that are easy to wash. (How many cartons of orange juice have you burst on an airplane?) Second, eat a good meal at least two hours before you fly and avoid eating too much on the flight itself. The reduced pressure restricts blood flow and makes digestion more difficult. Third, for the same reason, keep moving about to avoid cramps, and reduce the risk of DVT (Deep Vein Thrombosis) by walking around the cabin every hour or so and wiggling your feet regularly. Fourth, keep hydrated by drinking plenty of water and avoid drinking too much fruit juice or alcohol.

Jetlag

Beating jetlag is all about resetting your body clock. The first step is to set your watch to your destination time as soon as possible to encourage your body to do the same (see *www.timezoneconverter.com*). Avoid alcohol and sleeping pills as both will leave you feeling groggy and your body adjusts better on its own (this is particularly important if you are expecting to drive a hire car from the airport when you arrive). For longer flights, when jet lag is more severe, the earlier you start preparing yourself, the better. A good source of advice can be found at *www.bodyclock. com*, which shows you how to alter your routine in the run up to your flight in order to minimise the impact of the time change when you arrive.

Long-haul

When a flight seems like it's going on forever, get the world map open at the back of the in-flight magazine and break the journey down into sections. Every time you cross one of the boundaries reward yourself with a walk around the cabin or a light snack. Sleep is a great way to pass the time but if you can't drop off, keep yourself occupied with a puzzle or a good book and avoid those free movies. Before you know it, you'll be either snoozing happily or approaching your final descent. For smokers, nicotine replacements will help smooth the journey along.

Plane air

The cabin of an airplane isn't pressurised to sea level conditions and this is what makes air travel so tiring. The air is drier and of lower quality too, so you will need to keep well hydrated and boost your immune system with plenty of fresh fruit and vegetables and perhaps the odd vitamin supplement.

Contact lenses

If you use contact lenses, don't wear them on a flight as the dry air in the cabin will make them uncomfortable and difficult to remove. It's a good idea to keep them in your hand luggage though as the lower pressure in the hold can draw the solution out of the container and dry them to a crisp.

Nodding off

The secret to a good sleep on a journey is to recreate the conditions you normally sleep in at home: in a dark, quiet, comfortable place. This is not always easy but the trick is to use an inflatable neck cushion with ear plugs and eye shades. Be careful if you are carrying valuables though as sensory deprivation makes an easy street for pick-pockets.

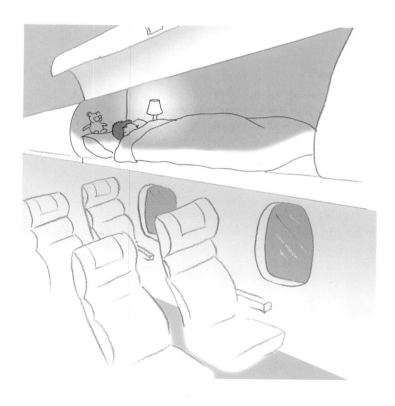

Slip on, slip off

Another effect of flying is that your feet swell up. If you keep your shoes on, by the time you touchdown your feet can be very uncomfortable. So it's a good idea to wear shoes that you can easily slip on and off. No one likes a wet sock when they visit the toilet!

Road trips

On long road trips the more traffic you encounter, the more tiring the drive will be, so adjust your stops accordingly. Water can be just as good at keeping a driver alert as coffee and it's important to keep well hydrated all the way. If you find drinking difficult while driving, use a bladder-type container with a hose attached (available from most camping stores) as you can safely drink from these hands-free and take smaller sips to cut down on toilet breaks.

Driving overseas

If you're going to be driving a car overseas, make sure you know the rules of the road beforehand as there are always anomalies. In the centre of Melbourne, Australia, for example, if you want to turn right at a cross roads you need to get into the far left hand lane and wait for the light to go green on the road to your immediate left before pulling out in front of the traffic to your right. Sound scary? It is. For a good source of advice, see *www.drivingabroad.co.uk*.

Bus journeys

Travelling by bus overseas is a great way to meet people. But security can be a problem so use a money belt for your valuables and keep it tucked beneath your clothes rather than out on show as it's a prime target. You should also keep your valuables on you rather than in the luggage compartment as it's been known for stowaways to board tourist buses and rifle through the bags below while everyone sleeps quietly above.

Best seat on the bus

Always go for the front. You will feel the bumps and corners a lot less and can get off and on a lot easier when it stops. It's also a good idea to work out which side the sun is on during the journey as an afternoon in direct sunlight can wither even the hardiest traveller.

Train journeys

Travelling by train is one of the most relaxing, most soporific ways to get around. But if you're travelling alone you don't want to have to keep checking your bags to see if they're still there every time the train stops. The solution is to carry a lock and chain to attach them to the rack, or a custom-made PacSafe mesh (see *www.pac-safe.com*) which will also make them slash proof. You'll sleep a lot easier knowing no one can get into your gear.

Cycling holidays

Cycling holidays are a fantastic way to see a country and get to know its people, but always check the weather conditions before you go. A bike is no way to travel in a monsoon. Training is also vital as a week in the saddle can really take its toll. For efficient riding, keep a smooth motion by peddling quickly in a high gear rather than peddling slowly in a low gear.

Sailing off into the sunset

As oil prices rise and we become more sensitive to the impact of air travel on the environment, travelling by boat is likely to make a real comeback. From yachts to freighters there are ships to suit every budget and every taste, and there is no better place to realise the old travelling philosophy that happiness is a journey, not a destination.

All at sea

Where there are boats, there are shaky sea legs. If you're prone to sea-sickness, the best way to avoid it is to stay outside on deck right from the start of the journey and keep your eyes focused on the horizon. This gives your brain a chance to adjust to the unexpected sway of the boat.

Tackling travel sickness

Ginger and peppermint are great natural remedies for travel sickness but if you're already feeling ill, the last thing you want is to be eating roots and leaves. Fresh air is the ticket to calming your stomach but if you can't get any, take long, slow, deep breaths instead as this stimulates a similar, balancing response in the nervous system. You should also keep your head raised and your eyes open.

Taxis

Taxis are notorious booby traps for travellers, with many horror stories of extra zeros added to fares and unwitting travellers being dropped off on the wrong side of town. But they're still a great way to get around and learn about a city. Who knows the place better than a cabbie, after all? First ask a local how much the journey should cost you, then choose a registered, metered cab, agree on your fare before you get in and write it down so the driver can acknowledge it. If they don't, find another cab.

Taxi fares

One of the things you always want to know when you arrive in a new airport is how much the taxi ride to the city will cost. The best way to find out is to ask the person sitting next to you on the plane. It's a fair bet that they've been there before and who knows, you may even get to share the ride.

Rickshaws and tuk-tuks

Cheap and fun to ride, three-wheeled rickshaws and 'tuk-tuks' in Asia were once a traveller's best friend. But be aware that they aren't all that safe on the roads and due to their novelty value they're often more expensive than regular taxis. It's essential to agree on a price before you set off and if the driver offers to show you his friend's shop on the way, politely but firmly decline (unless you want to go and see the shop of course). As a rule, if you need to get somewhere quickly and safely, it's probably best to avoid them.

Go by foot

An underground train or packed bus rarely gives the best view of a city so to see more of the place and get your bearings, go by foot instead. There is no better way to get to know it than from the ground up.

Go against the flow

Tourist attractions can become a bit of a treadmill at times, with people literally falling over each other to see the sights. To avoid the wandering herds, vary your routes from what's suggested in the guidebook (try walking them in reverse, for example) and ask a local if they'd suggest anywhere else you should see. Remember, a guidebook never tells the whole story.

Did you know?

The first flight was made in 1783 by the Montgolfier Brothers who, watched by onlooking Marie Antoinette and King Louis XVI of France, took a sheep, duck and cockerel with them into the sky in a hot air balloon.

Day 26

Chapter 6 - Travelling with the Family

The perfect family holiday

Always a tall order, but the best family holidays are those that have something for everyone. Think carefully about what every family member would enjoy before you book, and find something that caters for as many tastes as possible. Toddlers and teenagers can be the most difficult to satisfy so adjust your expectations accordingly.

Healthy eating

Good food is essential for a good family holiday. Your choice of destination should offer cuisine that you can all enjoy and be careful to avoid anywhere with questionable hygiene. Bacteria that are harmless to adults can be very dangerous to young children. To make sure everyone stays healthy, take multi-vitamins and hydration salts with you as back-up.

A photographic memory

Always carry photographs of your children on holiday (or email them to a web based account) in case you're ever separated and they become lost. Even if you're faced with an insurmountable language barrier, you can still give a perfect description to the police.

Flying with children

Many long-haul flights have games consoles plugged into the back of the seats but don't always count on them working. Wherever you're flying, pack plenty of games to keep the kids occupied and if they get restless give them a drink and a sweet to suck on. Not as a treat, but to help balance the cabin pressure that will be affecting their ears more than your own.

Ear planes

These are special, travel ear plugs designed to reduce pain during take-off and landing by using special filters to ease the pressure. You can get them from most travel shops and some chemists, but keep a good supply if you travel a lot as they only work for one or two journeys. Smaller sizes are available for children.

Safe journeys

If you are on a long journey with children and want to get some sleep, make sure you sit on the outside in an aisle seat so if they do need to get out, they'll have to wake you first and you'll always know where they are.

Home comforts

If you take young children on holiday it's a good idea to pack their pillow cases as well as a few of their favourite toys. The room will feel a lot more like home once you've got the toys on the bedside table and the pillow cases over the pillows. Make sure they are distinctive though as it's easy to forget them if they are the same colour as the sheets.

Family fees

One of the biggest drawbacks to a family holiday is that you're always travelling in peak season. You can reduce the cost by booking late but your choices may be limited, so whenever you book always ask for child discounts. They can be up to 10% less than the full price and remember, babies often travel free.

Peak season?

Sometimes the only thing peaking in peak season is the annual rainfall. Peak season is determined by the school holiday schedule not the best weather conditions, so make sure you get your money's worth by finding out exactly which season you'll be travelling into before you book. It's never a guarantee of good weather, but at least you're prepared.

Bring education to life

A great way to make lessons more interesting next year at school is to take the family to visit places that are covered on the syllabus. When you've seen sixty-year-old bombs lying unexploded next to the battlefields of the Somme, or walked the mountain paths crossed by Hannibal and his elephants, it brings the lesson to life. If you ever need to take the kids out of school for a holiday (and to avoid peak season prices), this might also persuade the teacher it's a good idea.

Carry on camping

Just the idea of camping can leave some of us in need of a holiday, but don't knock it until you've tried it! Firstly, it's a cheap way to go, and secondly, most campsites are well geared up for families, with pools, playgrounds and day nurseries ready to take on the kids. The other great thing about camping with the family is the camaraderie you find among other campers that you don't normally get in a hotel.

Kids' club

It's not just campsites that have fun facilities for kids. If, on your next holiday, you're looking for a bit of time off for yourself as well as for the children, let a resort or a cruise ship with a kids' club do its wonders for you. See websites like *www.childfriendly.co.uk* for advice.

Baby wipes

Not just for babies! They're an essential item for any trip but especially when you're travelling with the family. When you've been on the road for a long time, wet-wipes are a great way to freshen up. Hand sanitiser is also extremely useful, keeping your hands clean when there's no soap or water to wash them.

Family bags

Too much luggage can really slow you down on a family holiday – especially with young children. The best bet is to pack as much as you can into your own bags and make sure the youngest don't have to carry much at all. Backpacks with removable day-packs are ideal as you can attach your child's bag to your own when it gets too much for them.

Stop the squabbles

A good way to stop in-fighting on a long journey with children is to have a pick-n-mix bag of toys and treats to hand. Before anything gets too heated, hand the bag around and let the squabblers pick their own amusement.

Holiday scraps

Another way for the children to remember their holidays is to encourage them to collect local memorabilia like ticket stubs, visitor leaflets and postcards that they can compile into a scrapbook. Again, it's a good idea to buy the scrapbook when you arrive so they know what the project entails, and make sure they complete it before the flight home.

Creative genius

The relaxation time you get on holiday can be an inspired source of creativity, so why not capture some of it in a sketchbook on your next trip? Family drawings of the places you visit make better souvenirs than photographs.

Go the write way

Travel journals make bestsellers these days, so why not encourage the family to keep their own? Always buy the notebooks overseas as they are fantastic souvenirs and will make fascinating reading years later. Encourage your children to note down all the questions they have about the places they visit – not just the details – as this will inspire their natural curiosity. You never know, you might have another Bill Bryson on your hands.

A room with a view

We all want a hotel room with a view, but if you're travelling with children make sure the window can't be easily unlocked so they're not likely to fall out. Similarly if you have a balcony, as soon as you arrive make sure it's safe and fit for family use.

Don't be shocked

Electricity supplies are not always as safe overseas as they are at home so take care whenever using transformer plugs; always check the bathroom for any power points that could come into contact with water, and make sure all the heaters or air conditioning units have been properly safety tested before switching them on.

House swaps

A great way to take the family on holiday without losing all the conveniences of home is to arrange a house swap with a family from another country. It's cost effective and gets you away from the tourist traps. The cheapest way is to make your own arrangements with friends overseas, but agencies like *www.homelink.org.uk* and *www.homebase-hols.com* can also arrange things for you.

Top Ten Family Holidays

1. Camping on the south coast of France.
2. Keeping fit on a water sports holiday in the Mediterranean.
3. Exploring the ancient temples of Jordan.
4. Enjoying a traditional family Christmas in Finland.
5. Following the 500km Dinosaur Trail in Queensland, Australia.
6. Kayaking through the calm waters of Croatia's Dalmatian coast.
7. Mixing snorkelling with pyramids and camel safaris in Egypt.
8. Finding lost civilisations in the mountains of Peru.
9. Relaxing on the jungle-fringed beaches of Costa Rica.
10. Meeting the elephant orphans of Sri Lanka.

Chapter 7 –
Making the Most of Your Holiday

Hand washing

Washing your clothes by hand is not something we have to do very often these days, but it's very useful if you can do it well while travelling. The trick is good old fashioned elbow grease. It's no good leaving dirty clothes out in a bowl to sunbathe! You've got to get in there and give them a proper kneading. Take travel wash with you as some local brands contain bleach that's unsuitable for many fabrics.

Take a gift

If you live in Kendal, take mint cake. If you're from Kentucky, take bourbon! Something unique to your home - however ordinary it seems when you're there - takes on a completely different value overseas and will make a very special gift for someone you meet. In northern India, for example, Levi's jeans are highly valued.

Don't forget your roots

Take photos of your friends and family and even postcards of your home town with you on holiday. You might want to get away from it all, but the people you meet will be fascinated to see where you've come from, and the shared understanding will create an instant bond between you.

Writing home

Ever promised everyone a postcard and sent none? Give yourself a head start by printing address labels from your computer before you leave and then attach them to a set of postcards as soon as you arrive. You've got the whole holiday to write the messages and no excuse for not sending them!

Know your way

It's important you enjoy yourself on holiday, but not at the expense of the local way of life. What is permissible at home might not be overseas – like drinking in public or walking around without a shirt on – and it is your responsibility to be aware of local customs, not the other way round. Read a good country guide before you go to make sure you travel with respect.

Speak the language

The spread of the English language has made us much lazier travellers than we should be, but a little effort to speak the local language goes a very long way. One of the great joys of travelling is the opportunity to learn about another culture but if you speak English everywhere you go you can miss out on this entirely.

The right souvenirs

Be careful about the souvenirs you buy overseas. What appears to be in abundant supply in the market place could be an endangered species, a protected artefact, or even a substance that is banned back home, all of which will land you in hot water in Customs.

Sign language

Much less satisfying than learning to speak the lingo but if you find it hard to pick up a new language, draw pictures to help you communicate instead. If you're not good at drawing, either, no worries! Use an image search engine like Google Images to print them off before you go.

Take it easy...

In a hot climate, have you ever noticed the locals walking a lot slower than all the tourists? Or been surprised when you've arrived in a restaurant pouring with sweat when everyone else is bone dry? That's because you've been rushing around at the same pace you would back home! The hotter it is, the slower you need to go.

...Once more, take it easy!

Holidays are all about relaxing, but when things don't happen as quickly as you might expect, or don't run exactly to plan, don't sweat about it. The different pace of life is all part of the joy of travelling and you won't beat them, so just join them.

Plugging in

If you're travelling with a laptop and want to be able to connect to the internet, take an acoustic coupler with you. This will connect your modem to most telephone lines and will get you online almost anywhere in the world. Although whether a holiday with a laptop is really a holiday at all is another question…

Warming up

Adventure holidays can be physically demanding and none more so than skiing. To make sure you can still walk to the bar after a day on the slopes, do some warm-up exercises before you go. One of the best is to press your back against a wall with you legs bent perpendicular at the knee and…hold it for as long as you can.

Go local

If you travel thousands of miles to do all the same stuff you do at home, it's not really a holiday, is it? The best trips are when you go local, get into the way of life and broaden your horizons. Every culture has something to teach and something to learn from, and with that you're guaranteed a holiday to remember.

Volunteer work

Volunteering overseas is hard work but it's the best way to get to know another culture. It doesn't sound like much of a holiday but it could be the most refreshing, most enlightening break you ever take. Travel has a massive impact on culture and the environment, and as we move towards a more sustainable future it's going to become even more important that we give something back to the places we visit. See *www.responsibletravel.com*, *www.earthwatch.org* or *www.i-to-i.com*.

Leave no trace

Easier said than done, but leaving things the way you found them is not only respectful but increasingly vital as man's environmental impact takes hold. There's a question as to whether travel can ever be truly sustainable, but a good start would be to make your flight 'carbon neutral' by paying an organisation like *www.climatecare.org* to offset the emissions spent getting to your destination by planting trees and funding sustainable energy projects.

Taking photos respectfully

The photos you take of the people you meet abroad are always a treasure. But bear in mind that some cultures view photography very differently from us and you should always ask permission before snapping.

Top Twenty Cultural Tips

1. In France, don't bring a bottle. Supplying the wine for a friend's dinner party is not considered good taste, it implies that their own is not up to scratch.

2. South Korean food can be spicy but even if your nose runs, resist the temptation to wipe it! Using a handkerchief at the table is not polite.

3. In Pakistan, the left hand is reserved for the toilet so whenever paying someone or passing something to them, always use your right. This applies to food as well so unless you enjoy eating alone, never put food into your mouth with your left hand.

4. In Brazil, Turkey and Russia the OK sign (made with the thumb and index finger) is an obscenity and, unless you're looking for trouble, is best avoided.

5. In Bangladesh it's frowned upon for men and women to show affection in public but perfectly normal to see two men walking down the street holding hands.

6. In Muslim countries you should always take your shoes off when visiting mosques and people's houses. It also shows respect to keep your shoulders covered in public.

7. When giving flowers in Vietnam you should always give an even number, while in Bulgaria you should always give an odd number.

8. In many parts of the Middle East and Asia, the soles of the feet are taboo and should not be seen, shown or touched at any point.

9. In China, gifts are an important part of the culture but never give a clock as a present. Rather than being an attractive addition to the mantelpiece, it suggests you are counting the hours until the recipient's death.

10. In Japan, death is represented by the colour white so you should avoid giving gifts that are wrapped in white paper.

11. In Laos don't be surprised when you see men with long, manicured fingernails as they are very fashionable.

12. Throughout Asia, you will find you get a lot further when you keep your cool. If something is taking longer than expected, do not show your frustration as many cultures see this as 'losing face' and you will not be regarded with the same respect.

13. In South America, gesturing for someone to 'come here' by curling your fingers and palm towards your body is sexually suggestive and should be reserved for more private moments.

14. Never point with your finger in Indonesia - it's a rude gesture. Use your thumb instead.

15. In Greece, waving an open-palmed hand at someone to greet them can be offensive so it is best to keep your palm closed or facing in towards your body.

16. In Buddhist culture, the head is the most sacred part of the body and can only be touched by a close member of the family; never by a stranger.

17. In Thailand it's not a good idea to step on a bank note or even lick a postage stamp as both bear the King's head and this is a sign of disrespect.

18. In some remote parts of South East Asia countries, the camera lens is thought to capture a piece of the soul so you should always ask permission or offer payment before taking a photo and receiving this gift from people.

19. In Italy, you should never enter a church wearing shorts, a short skirt, or a vest. Your legs and upper arms should always be covered as a mark of respect.

20. In India, always get directions from several people as it can be considered more impolite to admit you do not know the answer than it is to give an incorrect answer.

Chapter 8 - Taking Better Photographs

Lights, camera, action

A holiday is one long photo-opportunity, so it's worth making the most of it. First, think about light. Light is the essence of a good photo and even the most mundane of subjects can shine in the right conditions. Remember that if your subject is between you and the sun, you won't pick out much detail, so keep the sun either behind you or to one side.

Dawn and dusk

The start and end of the day are golden times for the travel photographer. You'll find the most dramatic lighting with softer glows adds depth to colour, and character to the darker areas. If you take a photo in the middle of the day, think about where the sun will cast the heaviest shadow.

Good composition

A good trick to improve all your photos is to compose them in thirds rather than placing your subject right in the middle. This gives the finished product more balance and allows the background to become as interesting as the subject.

People shots

Despite the moans of the family, it's always a good idea to include people in your photos. Endless landscapes, however beautiful, can lose their appeal over time. With people in the foreground even a bad photo will tell you something about the experiences you shared.

One in the eye

Whenever you take photos of people or animals, always try to take them at their eye level. This is easy when your subject is the same height as you, but more difficult when you're taking photos of young children and especially animals. The results will be worth the effort though.

Level headed

It's easy to focus your attention on your subject and forget about what's behind them, but this often leads to a wonky horizon that can ruin the overall shot (especially when you're on a boat). To keep a level head on all your photos, make sure your horizon lines run parallel to the top and bottom of the frame.

Mini tripod

A mini tripod is a handy addition to the travel photographer's kit. With adjustable legs, you can get a level shot no matter how uneven the surface, and get more from your night time photos when longer shutter speeds demand a rock steady lens. Gorillapods are especially versatile, available from *www.amazon.com*.

Go digital

With high quality lenses, no film to carry and huge memory storage, digital cameras are ideal for travelling. They take great photos and the display screens make composition easier, while the review and delete options mean you only end up with the best photos. As well as saving space, the memory cards also mean you don't have to worry about sending exposed film through the x-ray at the airport.

Web Storage

The best place to keep your holiday photos is an online storage facility like *www.snapfish.com* or *www.kodak.com*. They are free, you can upload as many photos as you want, and email a link to your friends while you're still away so they can see what you're up to. When you want to order the prints, just choose the ones you want and they'll post them to your door.

Action Shots

The autofocus can slow a digital camera down just enough to miss an action shot so this is the time to go manual. You will have to anticipate the shot by having your camera switched on and preset to the right focal point, and then take the photo just before the event so the shutter opens at exactly the right moment.

Recharging your batteries

Despite the advantages, some photographers will tell you to avoid taking a digital camera on holiday as the batteries will run out long before your memory card and recharging them is a problem. It's more difficult than replacing an old lithium battery, but not insurmountable. Using a plug adapter is one option, but if your charger isn't made for the local voltage it can be unreliable. You could buy a new charger when you arrive - but they can be expensive and won't be any use back home. The solution is to take a car charging unit as the 12-volt adapter will work on almost any car cigarette lighter in the world.

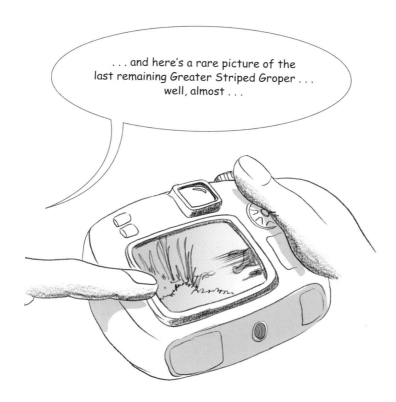

Selling your photos

Travel companies and travel magazines are always on the lookout for photos of stunning locations so don't be afraid to put your photos to work to help pay for your next holiday. If they're well composed, focused, and show something unique about the place you visited, they could become much more than holiday snaps. To find out whom to offer them to, go to your local newsagent and copy the phone number and editor's name from the front of the travel magazines and give them a call.

Happy snaps

Your camera is probably the most delicate item you take on holiday so make sure you get a decent case and sufficient insurance. Soft, durable bags are easier to carry but for complete safety go for a rigid, waterproof container.

Photographic boomerang

To give your camera the best chance of finding its way back to you, start your roll of film with a photograph of your home address with a note saying: 'please return if you find this camera!'

Did you know?

Photographs of deceased, indigenous Australians should not be shown for several years after their death out of respect.

Chapter 9 – Looking After Your Money

Money makes the world go round

They say money makes the world go round and that's definitely true where holidays are concerned. You should always change some currency before you go so you can familiarise yourself with the different denominations and be ready to use it as soon as you arrive.

Taking money abroad

The trick is to keep all the bases covered. Traveller's cheques are secure but to avoid heavy exchange charges you'll need large denominations, which can leave you with more cash than you'd like to carry around. ATMs have become a more viable alternative with reliable exchange rates, but the unpredictable fees can still give you a shock on the bank statement. In Britain, some banks don't charge for overseas transactions and if you do a lot of travelling, it's worth shopping around for the right account before you go. Finally, always take a credit or debit card abroad and make sure it is a well known brand like Visa or MasterCard.

Make a crib sheet

Print out an exchange rate crib sheet before you go abroad so you know at a glance how much you are paying. Make one column for your own currency and another for the local currency, and then list ten or twenty equivalent denominations side by side. Websites like *www.xe.com* or *www.x-rates.com* can give you the going rates.

Withdrawals

If you need to draw money on your bank account overseas, remember that most ATMs will charge you as well as your bank. To avoid paying twice use your card in a supermarket and ask for 'cash back' if the service is available. That way you should only pay for your money at the going exchange rate.

Safe exchange

Backstreet exchange booths may offer lower rates, but the difference is usually so minimal you have to change a lot of cash to make any real difference – which is not a risk you want to take down any backstreet! Stick to legitimate money changers in well lit, well policed areas.

Ready money

Many countries use American Dollars as secondary or even primary currency so before you fly find out if it's worth taking some. Unlike some local currencies, U.S. Dollars won't lose their value and can also be useful in an emergency. Take a range of denominations right down to one dollar bills.

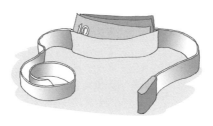

Small is beautiful

Small notes are always more useful, especially in developing countries where large denominations draw attention and can be hard to change. You should also avoid pulling out large wads of cash in public by planning ahead and preparing a stash of smaller notes for the day before you leave the hotel.

Bartering

Bartering is nothing to be ashamed of. In many countries it's a natural and respected part of buying and selling. But at the same time, remember that it's not a sport and shouldn't be done for its own sake. Before starting your negotiations, think how much you'd be willing to pay. If the price is lower than the figure in your head, you've already got a bargain. If the price is higher than you expected, as a rule of thumb, offer 50% and settle at around 75% of the total. Whenever buying expensive items do your research so you know the market rate.

Tipping

Tips are always hard to quantify so find out what the local custom is before you arrive and be ready to reward good service. More often than not, you'll end up getting better service as a result. A good source of advice can be found at *www.tipping.org*.

No money?

If you are overseas and you've been robbed of all your cash, the first place to go is your local embassy which should be able to arrange emergency funds, for a fee payable later. Another option is to speak to a company like Western Union or Money Gram who specialise in wiring money around the world.

Change on the street

If someone asks you to change a large note on the street, politely decline. This is a classic lead into a wallet snatch. Similarly, don't carry all your cash in one pocket and ideally, try to carry a second wallet with a few small notes in it that you are happy to hand over to a mugger without a second thought.

Did you know?

The islands of Yap in Micronesia have streets that are literally lined with money. For day-to-day transactions they use U.S. Dollars but the indigenous currency is still highly valued - cut from a limestone quarry and fashioned into circular, stone coins. Some of the coins are so large that they can't be moved and are left to adorn the pathways of local villages.

Chapter 10 - Travelling on a Budget

Book online

There are many good deals available online but look out for hidden extras. Tax isn't always included in the first price you're quoted and there may be restrictions on when and where you can travel. A quick way to compare prices is to use a 'metacrawler' like *www.airline-network.com*, *www.expedia.com* or *www.opodo.com*. But bear in mind that both prices and availability can change from day-to-day, from site-to-site. A flight that's fully booked one day, for example, can be available the next when a new carrier starts taking bookings.

Don't just fly mid-week, buy mid-week!

It's always cheaper to fly Wednesday-to-Wednesday than it is to fly Saturday-to-Saturday, but did you know it can also be cheaper to book your tickets midweek than at the weekend? It's all down to supply and demand and it stands to reason that travel companies are likely to set their prices higher when more people are making their bookings. For the same reason you should book your summer holidays at the end of the previous summer and your winter holidays at the end of the previous winter.

Leave it to chance

One of the best ways to get a cheap holiday is to leave your destination to chance and book the best-priced holiday a few days before you go. Weekend travel sections in the newspapers, and websites like *www.lastminute.com* can be good for deals and, in Britain, the TV Teletext service is still worth a look.

Free camping

Camping is one of the cheapest holidays going and did you know that in Britain it's even cheaper to pitch a tent in Scotland than it is in England and Wales? That's because north of the border you can camp 'wild' on public land away from roads and dwellings without having to pay any fees, while further south you are restricted to designated campsites. You won't have the luxury of camp facilities of course, but the pristine views more than make up for it. The golden rule, as ever, is to leave everything as you found it and take everything you brought with you back home again.

Sail away

If time is no object and you're feeling adventurous, one of the most cost-effective ways to see the world is to take a job on a ship: either by crewing a yacht or working on a cruise ship. It's hard work all the way, no doubt, but worth the effort when you arrive in your sun blessed destination with money to burn.

Get bumped

Many flights are overbooked by airlines on the expectation that a few passengers won't show up on the day. But every now and again everyone does show up on the day and there aren't enough seats. So if you're a budget conscious traveller and this happens on your flight, offer to get bumped onto the next as the airline will pay you for the inconvenience. The flipside of this is that if you do want to fly and you don't have a seat, this is your best chance to get a free upgrade to first class!

Student cards

If you're a student and you have a valid student card, always take it on holiday as many countries, particularly in Europe, give student discounts on numerous top tourist attractions. As a back up, you should also take an ISIC card (International Student Identification Card) which you can get from STA Travel (*www.isiccard.com*) and BUNAC (*www.bunac.org*). See *www.isic.org* for more information.

Travel further

Sometimes what you save on a cheap flight you spend as soon as you leave the airport, so to make sure your holiday stays on budget think about the cost of living in your destination before you book. You might spend more on the airfare but if you can live like royalty on a shoestring budget, it makes a lot of sense.

Work abroad

Some holidays will actually pay you for being there. The best known is TEFL (Teaching English as a Foreign Language) – which is particularly lucrative in the Middle East and Japan – but there are all kinds of ways to work your way around the world. You can arrange packages on the east coast of Australia, for example, where they teach you to sail before giving you a job as a sailing instructor. Speak to your local college or university about where to find a good TEFL course, and for jobs use *www.tefl.com*.

109

Call in all favours

If you have friends overseas and you want to save a bit of cash, arrange a holiday to go and visit them. Your wallet will be a lot happier and with a local to show you around, you'll get to see a lot more of the place than if you booked into a hotel.

Cook it yourself

Self-catered accommodation can be expensive up front, but once the costs are divided between everyone staying there and you factor in the savings made by not eating out for breakfast, lunch and dinner, you soon save a few bucks.

Cheaper transport

Another bill that mounts up fast on holiday is the cost of transport, especially if you have to get a taxi back to the hotel every night. There are three very simple ways round this: first, make sure your hotel is in walking distance from the major sights, if it's not, hire a bike, and finally use public transport as much as possible. That way you'll save money and meet more people at the same time.

Good training

Many countries offer discounts on long distance train journeys if you book in advance but hammer you on the ticket price if you buy it on the day of travel. In Europe, the best option is a Eurailpass; but wherever you are, always book direct with the train company to get the cheapest ticket and avoid commission.

Buy local

If you don't mind leaving things open to chance, try booking your holiday activities when you arrive rather than in advance. That way you'll save on booking fees knowing you're also supporting the local economy, which in many destinations relies on tourist income.

Get junk mail

It's time to stop hating junk mail because where holidays are concerned, it can save you a packet. First, set up a separate email address so your real address isn't affected, then sign up for as many different travel e-newsletters as possible. Your inbox fills up faster than a pint glass at Oktoberfest, but this is how tour operators shift their underbooked trips so you'll be the first to know about the bargains.

Take a stove

Food always makes a dent in the travel budget so why not take a camping stove with you and cook your own? As long as you've got good weather, it's ideal. What could be better than a steaming hot bowl of pasta with glass of wine on the beach as you watch the sun setting over the waves?

Travel by night

Accommodation is usually the single biggest cost on holiday, but if you travel at night you can sleep on the way. It's not a good idea for families, single travellers or business travellers, but if you're with a group of friends it's fine.

Take a sandwich course

Not so you can get a job in a snack bar, but a year for a student to live and work abroad while studying. It's a fantastic way to discover another culture, learn a new language and get great work experience at the same time.

Travel for a good cause

Another way to travel on the cheap is to give your time to a good cause when you get there. As well as helping people you'll be driving your cost-of-living way down. You could even fundraise for the trip beforehand to help with the cost and provide supplies for the project. To find a project, research the issues that are affecting the country and approach a local NGO (Non-Government Organisation) to see if they need help.

Use a sleeping sheet

If you're on a tight budget you may not be staying in the most luxurious of hotels, so it's a good idea to take a sleeping sheet with you. This could either be a bed sheet stitched together down one side, a duvet cover or custom-made sleeping bag liner. They can make even the most inhospitable bed feel more like home.

Did you know?

The Nazca Lines are 275 metre-long drawings of animals and geometric forms etched into the Peruvian desert which lay undiscovered for 1,500 years until the first plane flew over the area in 1927.

114

Chapter 11 - Keeping Healthy

Medical notes

Even if you are in perfect health you should always carry medical notes overseas with details of your blood type, any medication you're taking and any significant medical conditions you've had, preferably translated into the local language. If you need treatment it could save your life.

Emergency contacts

Another essential item to keep in a safe place is a list of emergency contacts. They should include your home address, your hotel address, your local Embassy, your next-of-kin and your airline or tour operator. If you get into trouble at least you, or someone else, will know who to call.

Free health insurance

In Europe many countries have reciprocal health agreements that allow travelling citizens to use their hospitals free of charge. British citizens can take advantage of this by completing an E111 form at the Post Office, but you should always have travel insurance as well. For those living outside Britain, contact your local health department or health insurer to see what you're covered for.

Travel insurance

Wherever you travel, don't leave home without good insurance. You should be insured for the loss of belongings, health care, legal bills, personal liability and, with security issues ever present, curtailment and cancellation. Always read the small print and remember that the best policies are rarely the cheapest. Websites like *www.moneysupermarket.com* or *www.confused.com* can help you compare what's on offer.

Wild at heart

If you're planning on taking a raft down a white water ravine or plunging off a bridge with only a rubber cord to save you from certain death, make sure your travel insurance covers you for it. Many policies include extreme sports but note that skiing and professional sports require special cover.

In an emergency

When you are a long way from home, you want to be sure that your insurance company can get you out of trouble – especially in a developing country – so ask what international assistance and emergency repatriation cover they provide. Don't just assume it's included. Find out which organisation they will liaise with (like *www.internationalsos.com*, for example) and whether this organisation operates where you're going to be.

117

Best laid plans

If you're booking with a tour operator, one of the things you're paying for is their responsibility to get you out of trouble if something goes wrong. Test how well prepared they are by asking what procedures they have in place to deal with an overseas emergency like a terrorist threat or natural disaster. If they are diligent, they will employ consultants like Docleaf (*www.docleaf.com*) to advise them and provide detailed contingency plans.

First aid kit

You should take a first aid kit on every trip, even if you're just heading off in the car for a weekend away. It should contain the following:

- pain killers
- tweezers
- stomach medicine
- anti-inflammatory tablets
- anti-histamine tablets
- antiseptic lotion
- plasters
- blister patches
- bandages
- thermometer
- matches (in a waterproof case)
- birth control pills
- condoms
- prescription medication (to last as long as you're away)

Safer jabs

If you're travelling to a country where resources are scarce – particularly the developing countries of Asia, South America and Africa – always take your own syringes and needles in case you're hospitalised and need an injection. This preserves local equipment and gives you the reassurance that yours is sterile. Always pack them in your checked luggage though.

Vaccinations and inoculations

Before you travel, be sure to check whether you require vaccinations, inoculations or preventative medication for diseases like Hepatitis, Yellow Fever or Malaria. In Britain, most are available free through the NHS but some, like the jabs for Rabies and Japanese Encephalitis, might only be available privately. To get an idea of what you need see *www.traveldoctor.co.uk*, but always remember to consult your doctor. Plan well ahead as some courses take several weeks to take effect.

Malaria

People say the best way to avoid Malaria is to not get bitten in the first place, but even for the most diligent repellent-sprayers, that's pretty unrealistic. If you're travelling to an area where the disease is prevalent, be sure to take the correct medication (see your doctor for advice) and don't believe for a minute the old yarn about the tablets simply masking the disease; anti-malarials effectively inhibit its development and the last thing you want is full blown malaria.

Mosquitoes

The active ingredient in most mosquito repellents is a chemical called 'diethyl-m-toluamide' or DEET for short. If you are travelling in the tropics, or any area where there are disease-carrying mosquitoes, use a repellent with at least 50% DEET concentration. However, don't rely on DEET alone as it's not 100% effective and can be harmful when used over prolonged periods (especially to children). Keep covered as much as possible and avoid being outside at dawn and dusk when the bugs are most active.

Natural alternatives

The best natural mosquito repellent is citronella oil. Less harmful and often cheaper than DEET, it is ideal for longer trips when you'll be living with the mossies night after night. To stop you dreaming of helicopters buzzing in your ears, take a fine mesh mosquito net that's been treated in repellent to hang over your bed.

Zap don't scratch

If mosquito bites send you scratch crazy you've got three solutions. The first is to take an anti-histamine tablet, but these often make you drowsy so they're not always practical. Another option is to use aloe vera gel to naturally soothe the skin. By far the most effective solution, however, is a special mosquito bite 'zapper' which sends a tiny, perfectly safe, electrical pulse through the bite to satisfy the itch, stop you from scratching, and prevent scarring. Available from *www.nomadtravel.co.uk*.

Sun stroke

There's something even worse than getting sand in your swimming trunks on the beach, and that's getting sun stroke. To avoid it, stay hydrated, keep your skin covered and keep out of direct sunlight. If you develop a headache, nausea, dizziness, high fever and small pupils, get help and call a doctor immediately. Emergency treatment can be administered by getting into a cold bath and pressing a cold towel into the back of your neck.

After sun

Not something you want to get caught without on a sunny holiday. There are many types of after sun and the best contain both aloe vera and mosquito repellent. When sun burn is at its worst, there's nothing quite as soothing as aloe vera; and nothing quite as painful as putting on stingy mosquito repellent afterwards!

Aloe, aloe, aloe

Pure aloe vera gel is one of the most versatile travel cosmetics going. You can use it as a moisturiser, after sun, burn ointment, shaving cream and even hair gel. If you're going where the sun shines, don't leave home without it.

Over enjoying

No matter where you travel, there's usually a morning after a night of drinking too much. Curing a hangover is all about getting rehydrated, but in a hot climate it can be hard to take in enough water to make up the deficit. To get the salts you need to sort you out, supplement your water intake with a rehydration sachet.

Make mine an H_2O

Most of us don't drink enough water when we're at home, but when we travel to a hotter climate than we are used to, it's even harder to drink as much as we need. In the tropics, you might need as many as 15 litres a day. Be careful though as too much water can be as dangerous as too little.

Diarrhoea

This is the most common of all travel ailments. Antimotility medication like Imodium is essential for journeys and will stop you from losing too much water. The body will often recover quickly on its own so the most important thing you can take is water and rehydration salts. A very effective stomach medicine is Pepto-Bismol which treats indigestion, nausea and diarrhoea, and kills bacteria. If your symptoms don't clear up in 72 hours or you have a fever, see a doctor.

Altitude sickness

Altitude sickness generally occurs above altitudes of 3,000 metres but everyone has a different level of tolerance. Symptoms include headache, dizziness and nausea leading to vomiting, insomnia and in extreme cases, cerebral or pulmonary oedema. The only really effective treatment is to descend. Before travelling to a mountainous region, find out how high the destination airport is, as some – like La Paz in Bolivia – are high enough to induce altitude sickness the moment you touch down.

DVT

Deep Vein Thrombosis hit the headlines as 'economy class syndrome' but it can happen in any type, and class, of journey – not just on airplanes. A blood clot forms within a vein, usually deep within the leg, which is rare but potentially fatal. Taking regular walks, avoiding sleeping for too long when sitting upright, taking aspirin, keeping well hydrated and keeping the blood moving by raising your heels and wiggling your toes regularly will all help avoid it.

Top Ten Adrenalin-Rush Holidays!

1. Heli-skiing in the Himalayas.
2. Venturing into the cloud forests of Ecuador.
3. Horse trekking in the American North West.
4. Driving a 4 x 4 through the Kimberleys in Western Australia.
5. Grizzly bear spotting in Alaska.
6. White water rafting in Zambia.
7. Hill walking on the south island of New Zealand.
8. River canoeing in the Canadian wilderness.
9. Venturing into the jungles of Borneo to see the Orangutans.
10. Riding a camel across the Kalahari Desert.

Chapter 12 - Staying Safe

X-ray vision

Most airport security scanners are safe for both camera film and laptops but it's always worth checking with the personnel standing by them if you're in any doubt. Something to watch with these items, though, is the conveyor belt at the other end because even under airport CCTV cameras, it can be a hunting ground for thieves.

Tamper-proof bags

You can be separated from your bags for a long time when you travel so it's a good idea to make sure they are locked and secure. At best, if the security staff need to search your bag they will simply break open the lock and leave you a sticker to let you know. At worst, if someone has tampered with your bag and planted something in it (this has happened), you'll know as soon as you collect it and can alert the police before it goes any further.

Culture shock

Ever felt totally bewildered in the first few hours of arriving in a new country? That's culture shock. It's a natural reaction, but it can also leave you disoriented and vulnerable to people who don't have your best interests at heart. To beat it, have a plan of attack when you first arrive, know your destination and pre-book your onward travel plans to give you somewhere to head to. It may cost you a bit more up front, but the security and peace of mind are well worth it.

Don't forget the padlocks

It's a good idea to use a bag with zips that are designed to be locked with padlocks for security. Combination locks give you fewer keys to lose, but if you use more than one don't set them all to the same code as this makes it twice as easy for someone to figure it out. Of course this means it's twice as hard to remember them as well, but if memory is a problem, email the codes to a web-based email account.

Secure baggage labels

If your bags go missing in transit you don't want someone to get your name and address from the label and know you're not at home. A safer alternative is to use a service like *www.bagsreunited.com* or *www.yellowtag.com* that will register your details on their database and issue you with a unique label that means your bags can be returned to you without your personal details being compromised.

Tie a yellow ribbon

A brightly coloured ribbon tied around your bags will make them much easier to spot on the baggage reclaim – especially if your suitcase is square and black like all the rest.

Remove the old labels

If you do a lot of travelling and you still have the old baggage labels attached from your previous flight, make sure you remove them before checking your bags onto your next flight. Otherwise they could be doing a lot more travelling than you!

Jewellery

Leave all the good stuff at home. Wearing expensive jewellery when you travel makes you a magnet to thieves who know immediately that you have more money than most. Furthermore, travel insurance rarely covers single, expensive items.

Don't give them a chance

It's easy to become a target on holiday so don't make it easy for pickpockets by leaving your valuables on show. Small rucksacks are easy to unzip as you walk along unaware, so if you do leave a camera or something valuable in there, make sure the bag is secure. Specially designed, lockable zips are advisable.

Hide your security wallet

Security wallets, or money belts, are useful as long as they are kept out of sight in public at all times. If yours is on show it's immediately obvious that you're carrying all your cash on you and it's all too easy for someone to cut the straps and walk away. If you need to get money from it, do it discreetly where you can't be seen.

Make it a chest strap

When you travel, you should wear any single-strap bag across your chest. If you leave it loosely slung over one shoulder it's easy to swipe. You should also make sure the strap is sturdy enough to resist a knife slash.

Keep an eye on your passport

Even more than your airfare, your passport is your ticket home. Losing your passport overseas is a headache to be avoided at all costs. Whenever hiring a car, for example, always try to leave something else as a deposit because your passport could be worth more on the black market than the car itself. In hotels it can be hard to avoid leaving your passport but if you can leave a driving licence instead, do.

Check it out before you check in

When you arrive in a hotel, always ask to see the room before you check in. They are less likely to palm you off with a bad room and if they refuse, you know to go somewhere else straight away. Unless a disability prevents you from doing so, it's also safer to get a room on the first or second floor rather than the ground.

Take your room key

It's not a good idea to leave your room keys behind reception in a hotel as it advertises that you're not there to look after your stuff. The same goes for 'Please Clean My Room' signs – it's much better to use 'Please Do Not Disturb' and clean it yourself.

Wedge it

A good way to sleep safe and sound is to take a door wedge with you and place it beneath the door at night time. Even if someone gets past the lock, you know they're not getting any further without waking you up.

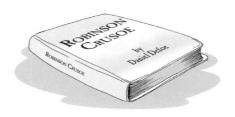

Taxi scam

To avoid losing everything when a taxi driver drives away, never pay for your fare until you have collected all your belongings from the cab.

Hire car scam

It's been known for car jackers to deliberately drive into hire cars and, as soon as the bewildered tourist gets out to inspect the damage, to jump in and drive off with all their belongings. If you're ever involved in an accident in a hire car overseas, stay put, get the other person's details, and go straight to the police.

Buy now, pay later

Never fall for this one. Always pay upfront and get a receipt. If you're paying for a service in advance, it's essential you get all the inclusions written down and signed by the tour operator providing them. That way you won't be short changed or landed with an unexpected price hike.

Getting the right directions

Try to get directions from public officials as they are less likely to send you the wrong way. If there's none around, ask more than one person for the same directions, just to be sure.

Finding your way around

Maps are an essential travel item but don't pull them out in confusion on a street corner as this will make you a target for thieves. Instead, study your map back at the hotel and figure out the key landmarks that will show your way home. The skyline gives the best pointers so look up as soon as you leave the hotel and take note of what's around you.

Going it alone?

When you travel alone, always tell someone where you're going, even if it's just the receptionist at the hotel. That way, if you get lost and find yourself in need of rescue, the emergency services can always trace your steps. Take a business card from the hotel with you as well.

Shortcuts

Avoid them at all costs. When you don't know a city, what looks like a good shortcut can quickly leave you lost in a dodgy part of town. Stick to the main routes.

Face-on

Whenever walking on the roads, face into the traffic so you can see what's coming and you're not at risk of cars pulling up behind you. It's also a bad idea to stereotype pickpockets. They can be young or old, male or female and it always happens when you least expect it.

Register at the embassy

If you're travelling to a high risk country where security is an issue, it's a good idea (and sometimes mandatory) to register at your embassy as soon as you arrive so you can be accounted for if anything happens. Similarly, if you lose everything on holiday – bags, passport, the lot - you should contact your embassy or consular services immediately to obtain temporary travel documentation and emergency cash.

Emergency power

Some of us take a break to get away from our mobile phones, but for those who can't leave home without them, you need never worry about a flat battery again: Eurohike have an ingenious solution: a wind-up torch with a mobile phone charger attached. Available from *www.millets.co.uk*.

Take a carabiner

If you've never been rock climbing you may not have encountered a carabiner before but they are an excellent travel security item. It is a metal loop with a sprung or screwed gate and is the quickest, safest way to make sure your bags don't get snatched. In a train station restaurant, for example, use a carabiner to attach the straps of your bags to the table leg so if someone tries to make a grab-and-dash, they'll end up taking the furniture and ketchup with them as well.

The Farthest Reaches of the World

1. The closest point on earth to the sun is an extinct volcano on the equator in Ecuador, known as Chimborazo, rising 6267 metres above sea level.

2. The lowest point on earth is the Dead Sea in the Middle East, 400 metres below sea level.

3. The wettest place in the world is Mawsynram in India which gets a staggering 12 metres of rainfall every year.

4. The driest place in the world is the Atacama Desert in Chile which, on average, receives less than a millimetre of rain a year.

5. The world's largest living structure is the 2000 kilometre Great Barrier Reef off the north east coast of Australia.

6. The world's most remote inhabited place is Easter Island, 4000 kilometres off the west coast of South America.

7. The world's oldest rainforest is the 130 million-year-old Taman Negara near Kuala Lumpur in Malaysia.

8. The world's most recently discovered species of mammal is the Muntjac Deer, found in Vietnam in 1994.

9. The largest festival in the world is India's Kumbha Mela which attracts over 10 million people.

10. The world's longest river is the 6680 kilometre Nile in Africa, but the world's largest river is the Amazon in South America, which holds a fifth of the entire world's fresh water.

Travel Checklist

Apart from the necessary clothing and toiletries and depending on your trip, the following list will prove useful…

- Valid passport
- Valid visa (if required)
- Travel tickets and itinerary
- Travel company contact details
- Travel insurance details
- Accommodation booking details / reference numbers
- Driving licence
- Car rental booking details / reference number
- Travel guide and phrase book
- Notebook, pen and calculator
- Cash (your currency and that of destination)
- Traveller's cheques
- Credit card
- Money belt
- Luggage labels (outward and return)
- Camera (with films or data card) and mini camera tripod
- Video camera (with films)
- Charged and/or spare batteries for cameras
- Electrical adapters appropriate for destination
- Binoculars
- Torch with new batteries (a head torch is preferable)
- Travel alarm clock
- Travel sickness pills
- A good book
- Sunglasses
- Sun screen and after sun / sunburn lotion
- Salt replacement sachets
- Water purifying tablets
- Carbohydrate snacks (in case of travel delays)

- Mirror
- Sewing kit and safety pins
- Basic first aid items including aloe vera gel
- Insect repellent spray or lotion and insect bite cream
- Mosquito net
- Eye shades and ear plugs
- Sarong
- Flip flops
- Travel towel (very absorbent)
- Wet wipes
- Re-sealable or zip-lock sandwich bags
- Backpack rain cover and waterproof stuff sack
- Duct tape (fixes everything!)
- Fishing line (strongest string in the world!)
- Swiss Army knife or Leatherman tool (packed in case NOT hand luggage)

Also remember to…

- Have inoculations if required (arrange these in plenty of time)
- Let relatives know how to contact you in case of emergency
- Tell friends / neighbours the length of your absence
- Arrange for care of pets in your absence
- Cancel milk, newspaper and other regular deliveries but NOT by doorstep note

Country Facts

Country	Capital	Official Language	Currency	Time Zone	Why Visit?
Australia	Canberra	English	Australian dollars	+8 to +10	Australia has some of the most unique wildlife, landscapes and indigenous culture in the world.
Bahamas	Nassau	English	Bahamian dollar	-5	Of 700 Bahamian islands, only 30 are inhabited.
Belize	Belmopan	English	Belizean dollar	-6	In a world where old growth rainforest is in rapid decline, two thirds of the original Belizean rainforest remains.
Bolivia	La Paz	Spanish	Boliviano	-4	Bolivia is a country of other worldly landscapes, none less so than the Altiplano salt flats; 4,000 metres up in the Andean mountains.
Brazil	Brasilia	Portuguese	Real	-3 to -4	Larger than the United States, Brazil has everything from cosmopolitan cities to ecology that is still unknown to man.

Cambodia	Phnom Penh	Khmer	Riel	+7	The Ankor Wat temple complex in Cambodia is one of the architectural wonders of the world; partly submerged in the tangled roots of banyan trees.
Canada	Ottawa	English/ French	Canadian dollars	-4 to -9	Canada is the world's second largest country with laid back cities, wild back country and great skiing.
Chile	Santiago	Spanish	Chilean peso	-4	Over just a few hundred kilometres in Chile you can travel from the coast to the desert to snow capped Andean mountains.
China	Beijing	Mandarin	Yuan	+8	China is home to the world's oldest surviving civilisation, which invented the abacas, the compass and the earliest printing techniques.
Costa Rica	San Jose	Spanish	Costa Rican colon	-6	Costa Rica is Central America's most accessible destination with jungle-fringed beaches and striking ecological diversity.
Croatia	Zagreb	Croatian	Kuna	+1	Croatia's Adriatic islands offer some of the best sailing in the world.

Country	Capital	Official Language	Currency	Time Zone	Why Visit?
Cuba	Havana	Spanish	Cuban peso	-5	Cuban music is legendary and the Caribbean's largest island will open your eyes to a completely different way of life.
Czech Republic	Prague	Czech	Czech koruna	+1	The Czech Republic is a timeless destination famed for its cobbled backstreets and bohemian culture.
Ecuador	Quito	Spanish	US dollar	-5	Ecuador's primeval landscape is home to some of the world's most important ecosystems.
Egypt	Cairo	Arabic	Egyptian pound	+2	The great pyramids of Egypt are testimony to one of history's greatest civilisations.
Estonia	Tallinn	Estonian	Kroon	+2	In Estonia you can enjoy medieval architecture by day and lively bars by night.
Fiji	Suva	Fijian	Fiji dollar	+12	Built on a series of extinct volcanoes that rise from the ocean floor, Fijian culture and customs have remained unchanged for generations.
France	Paris	French	Euro	+1	Go to France to indulge in some of the world's best food and wine.

Germany	Berlin	German	Euro	+1	From Einstein to Goethe, Germany is the birthplace of some of the world's greatest minds.
Greece	Athens	Greek	Euro	+2	Best known for its Mediterranean islands, Greece is also recognised as the birthplace of Western civilisation.
Honduras	Tegucigalpa	Spanish	Lempira	-6	The Bay Islands, off the north coast of Honduras, are the cheapest place in the world to learn to scuba dive.
Iceland	Reykjavik	Icelandic	Icelandic krona	GMT	Iceland is an isolated volcanic retreat in the North Atlantic where you'll find everything from whale watching to white water rafting.
India	New Delhi	Hindi	Indian rupees	+5½	Home to a rich variety of culture, India is one of the cheapest travel destinations going.
Indonesia	Jakarta	Bahasa	Indonesia rupiah	+7 to +9	In Indonesia you'll find great food, ancient heritage, exotic wildlife and 10% of the world's remaining tropical rainforest.
Ireland	Dublin	English	Euro	GMT	Ireland's wild coastline, lively pubs and welcoming hosts make it a first class destination.

Country	Capital	Official Language	Currency	Time Zone	Why Visit?
Italy	Rome	Italian	Euro	+1	Italian art and music have influenced global culture for hundreds of years.
Jamaica	Kingston	English	Jamaican dollar	-5	Home to one of the world's most influential styles of popular music, the reggae-infused island of Jamaica also grows some of the world's best coffee.
Japan	Tokyo	Japanese	Yen	+9	Japan is a curious mix of frenetic cities and gentle cultural traditions.
Jordan	Amman	Arabic	Jordanian dinar	+2	In Jordan you'll find the enigmatic 'lost' city of Petra, hand-cut from the arid, rocky landscape.
Kenya	Nairobi	Kiswahili	Kenya shilling	+3	A wildlife safari in Kenya is made all the more spectacular by the Great Rift Valley backdrop.
Madagascar	Antananarivo	Malagasy	Malagasy franc	+3	On the world's fourth largest island, every native mammal in Madagascar is endemic.
Malawi	Lilongwe	English	Malawian kwacha	+2	Malawi is one of Africa's most compact, accessible and varied destinations.

Country	Capital	Language	Currency	Time	Description
Malaysia	Kuala Lumpur	English	Ringgit	+8	Parts of the Malaysian rainforest are older than any other in the world.
Mauritius	Port Louis	English / French	Mauritian rupee	+4	Mauritius was described by Mark Twain as being a blueprint for heaven.
Mexico	Mexico City	Spanish	Mexican peso	-6	The Mayan and Aztec temples of Mexico were built by two of history's most dynamic civilisations.
Morocco	Rabat	Arabic	Moroccan dirham	GMT	In Morocco you'll find a heady mix of bustling marketplaces, rugged mountains and intricate Islamic architecture.
Mozambique	Maputo	Portuguese	Metical	+2	For isolated, stunning and accessible beaches, head to the coast of Mozambique.
Nepal	Kathmandu	Nepalese	Nepalese rupee	+5¾	Nepal is home to eight of the world's ten highest peaks, walked by the hardy Gurkhas and Sherpas for generations.
New Zealand	Wellington	English	New Zealand dollars	+12	New Zealand is an adventure sports playground maturing into one of the world's top wine producers.

Country	Capital	Official Language	Currency	Time Zone	Why Visit?
Norway	Oslo	Norwegian	Norwegian krone	+1	The Norwegian wilderness runs right down to its dramatic fjord-cut coastline, while its capital brims with art, music and culture.
Peru	Lima	Spanish	New sol	-5	Peru is one of the most environmentally diverse countries in the world, where you'll also find the famous Incan city of Machu Pichu.
Seychelles	Victoria	English/French	Seychelles rupee	+4	The Seychelles are 115 coral islands surrounded by clear, calm seas.
South Africa	Pretoria	Afrikaans	Rand	+2	South Africa is an accessible destination where you can enjoy as much wildlife in the city as you can in the national parks.
Spain	Madrid	Spanish	Euro	+1	Spain has many attributes but the highlight is Barcelona: acknowledged as one of the best cities in the world.
Sri Lanka	Colombo	Sinhala/Tamil	Sri Lankan rupee	+6	The tropical, bitesize island of Sri Lanka is a good destination for families and independent travellers.

Switzerland	Bern	German	Swiss francs	+1	Sedate travellers in Switzerland enjoy the picturesque cities and refined culture while the adrenalin-hunters hit the action in the Alps.
Tanzania	Dodoma	English	Tanzanian shilling	+3	Tanzania's ethnic diversity is magnificent, as is Kilimanjaro: the highest peak in Africa.
Thailand	Bangkok	Thai	Baht	+7	Thailand is an easy going destination with an open culture, great food and fantastic beaches.
Turkey	Ankara	Turkish	Turkish lira	+2	Turkey is often noted as a confluence of continents and for good reason: it is a fascinating slice of life and culture.
United Kingdom	London	English	Pound sterling	GMT	The UK is a historian's treasure chest with relaxing countryside retreats and influential urban culture.
United States	Washington DC	English	American dollars	-5 to -8	The U.S. caters for every travel taste with remote of America environments and glamorous, fast- paced cities.
Vietnam	Hanoi	Vietnamese	Dong	+7	Vietnam is an inexpensive place to enjoy world heritage environments and great ethnic diversity.

International Clothing Sizes

Men

Suits, Coats & Sweaters:

US	36	38	40	42	44	46
UK	36	38	40	42	44	46
European	46	48	51	54	56	59

Shirts:

US	14	14½	15	15½	16	16½	17
UK	14	14½	15	15½	16	16½	17
European	36	37	38	39	41	42	43

Shoes:

US	7½	8	8½	9½	10½	11½
UK	7	7½	8	9	10	11
European	40½	41	42	43	44½	46

Socks:

US	9½	10	10½	11	11½	12
UK	9½	10	10½	11	11½	12
European	39	40	41	42	43	44

Hats:

US	$6^5/_8$	$6^3/_4$	$6^7/_8$	7	$7^1/_8$	$7^1/_4$	$7^3/_8$	$7^1/_2$
UK	$6^1/_2$	$6^5/_8$	$6^3/_4$	$6^7/_8$	7	$7^1/_8$	$7^1/_4$	$7^3/_8$
European	53	54	55	56	57	58	59	60

Women

Suits & Dresses:

US	8	10	12	14	16	18
UK	10	12	14	16	18	20
European	38	40	42	44	46	48

Blouses & Sweaters:

US	34	36	38	40	42	44
UK	36	38	40	42	44	46
European	42	44	46	48	50	52

Shoes:

US	6	6½	7	7½	8	8½
UK	4½	5	5½	6	6½	7
European	37½	38	39	39½	40	40½

Children's Clothes:

US	4	6	8	10	12	14
UK (Ht inches)	43	48	55	58	60	62
European (Ht cm)	109	122	140	147	152	157

Temperature conversions

Celsius °C	Fahrenheit °F	Celsius °C	Fahrenheit °F
-30°C	-22°F	16°C	60.8°F
-20°C	-4.0°F	17°C	62.6°F
-10°C	14.0°F	18°C	64.4°F
0°C	32.0°F	19°C	66.2°F
1°C	33.8°F	20°C	68.0°F
2°C	35.6°F	21°C	69.8°F
3°C	37.4°F	22°C	71.6°F
4°C	39.2°F	23°C	73.4°F
5°C	41.0°F	24°C	75.2°F
6°C	42.8°F	25°C	77.0°F
7°C	44.6°F	26°C	78.8°F
8°C	46.4°F	27°C	80.6°F
9°C	48.2°F	28°C	82.4°F
10°C	50.0°F	29°C	84.2°F
11°C	51.8°F	30°C	86.0°F
12°C	53.6°F	40°C	104°F
13°C	55.4°F	50°C	122°F
14°C	57.2°F	60°C	140°F
15°C	59.0°F		

To convert Fahrenheit to Centigrade: $C = 5/9 \times (F-32)$

To convert Centigrade to Fahrenheit: $F = (9/5 \times C) + 32$

Index

Index

Index

'The Greatest Tips in the World' Books

Also available:

ISBN 9781-905151-02-8
Pub Date: Sept 2005

ISBN 9781-905151-03-5
Pub Date: Sept 2005

ISBN 9781-905151-04-2
Pub Date: Sept 2005

ISBN 9781-905151-05-9
Pub Date: Sept 2005

ISBN 9781-905151-06-6
Pub Date: Oct 2004

ISBN 9781-905151-07-3
Pub Date: April 2006

ISBN 9781-905151-08-0
Pub Date: April 2006

ISBN 9781-905151-09-7
Pub Date: April 2006

ISBN 9781-905151-10-3
Pub Date: April 2006

ISBN 9781-905151-11-0
Pub Date: Sept 2006

ISBN 9781-905151-12-7
Pub Date: Sept 2006

ISBN 9781-905151-13-4
Pub Date: Sept 2006

ISBN 9781-905151-22-6
Pub Date: Dec 2006

ISBN 9781-905151-25-7
Pub Date: April 2007

ISBN 9781-905151-30-1
Pub Date: April 2007

ISBN 9781-905151-18-9
Pub Date: May 2007

ISBN 9781-905151-19-6
Pub Date: June 2007

ISBN 9781-905151-21-9
Pub Date: June 2007

ISBN 9781-905151-17-2
Pub Date: August 2007

ISBN 9781-905151-28-8
Pub Date: Sept 2007

With many more to follow, these books will form a most useful compilation for any bookshelf.

'The Greatest in the World' DVDs

'The Greatest in the World - Gardening Tips' -
presented by Steve Brookes.

'The Greatest in the World - Yoga Tips' -
presented by David Gellineau and David Robson.

'The Greatest in the World - Cat & Kitten Tips' -
presented by Joe Inglis

'The Greatest in the World - Dog & Puppy Tips' -
presented by Joe Inglis

For more information about currently available and
forthcoming 'Greatest in the World' book and DVD titles
please visit:

www.thegreatestintheworld.com

or write to:

Public Eye Publications
PO Box 3182
Stratford-upon-Avon
Warwickshire CV37 7XW
United Kingdom

Tel / Fax: +44(0)1789 299616
Email: info@publiceyepublications.co.uk

The Author

Growing up in Britain in the eighties, Simon Worsfold was fortunate enough to travel all over the world at a young age: spending his winters skiing and his summers wherever the sun shone better than home.

As soon as he was old enough to go it alone, he branched out and ventured further afield to India, Nepal and southern Africa before settling into two years working for a travel company that sends volunteers to projects around the world. This only aggravated the travel bug and before long he left with his American girlfriend (whom he later married) to spend a year in Australia and South East Asia. From here he wrote a regular travel advice column for Verge magazine, based in Canada.

After all this, aged twenty seven, Simon still says there's nothing quite as exciting as the feeling of being pressed into the back of an airline seat when the pilot puts the throttle down for take off, and with close family in both Australia and the United States, this looks set to continue.

the worst ALBUM COVERS in the world 2

Nick DiFonzo

CONTENTS

INTRODUCTION

There has been a recent surge of interest in album cover artwork. There are now dozens of books and websites devoted to the finest examples of this popular arm of commercial artwork, covering everything from country to classic rock. Not only is record sleeve packaging now considered legitimate in the art world, with showings at major galleries, but the Average Joe MP3 seems to be noticing them as well. Despite this, album cover art is, to all intents and purposes, a dead medium. The compact disc was the beginning of the end, as the cover was shrunken and simplified. Now, most new music is downloaded and played without a thought given to any kind of permanent visual accompaniment whatsoever. Is it really so surprising then that album covers are being discovered by a generation that has never owned any?

Fuelling this trend, many young people across the world have taken 20th century pop culture nostalgia and turned it into an obsession. It's no secret that vintage is cool – a glance at any online auction site will tell you that. But sometimes we seem to have a selective memory of pop culture history. Our modern incarnations of 'the good old days' aren't always as accurate as we'd like to think! Popular throwback

RIGHT: From singing policemen to crooning drug addicts, no group was too odd to have an album!

THE ADDICTS SING

Nine former addicts

RIGHT: Some records manage to be shocking and heartwarming at the same time.

entertainment like *Austin Powers* or *That '70s Show* shows how great attention is paid to the accuracy of clothing, furniture, and the paint palette, while the themes, characters, and dialogue are purely modern. Cheap television documentaries re-use the same tired stock footage to portray the time period in question, while everyday events at which cameras were not present are forgotten.

Consider our modern image of the era most simply referred to as 'The '60s'. According to popular lore, everyone under the age of 25 was a hippie. The youth of America were on drugs. Hoards of odiferous teens regularly traversed the country in flower-bedecked buses from one rock festival to the next, stopping periodically to bathe naked in farmers' ponds. The generation was full of political activism: when not sticking flowers in soldiers' rifles, they were getting knocked down by fire hoses at a civil rights march. Ah, the '60s!

What does all of this have to do with album covers? More than you might think. We should all remember that our popular images of cultural

5

history aren't always giving us the whole story. For example, if every kid in the '60s was a free-loving communist hippie, then how do you explain the seemingly endless number of albums from young religious acts that were touring the country at the same time? Likewise, the popular notion of the wholesome home and family of the '50s does little to explain the suggestive sexuality of so many popular records of the time.

The point is that a good deal can often be learned about 'popular culture' by studying its unpopular aspects. Many of the artists and albums shown in this book were never very well-known. Some probably gave away more records than they ever sold. Others were quite well known in their day, at least in certain circles, but by now their names and records have both been relegated to the cut-out bin of history. Does that make their contributions any less important?

Often our cultural memories are dictated by modern economics. Of course everyone still remembers The Beatles, Elvis and The Rolling Stones – they are still economically viable 'product', making millions for record companies, estates and copyright holders. Meanwhile, countless other artists who did their share to contribute to cultural history remain unknown, simply because they no longer have the power to make money for other people.

Happily, there is hope for the chronically forgotten. The new possibilities of worldwide instant information access offered by the Internet assures that nothing will ever be completely forgotten again. From music to art to cinema

LEFT: Records from foreign countries are sometimes a great insight into another culture... And sometimes not so much.

RIGHT: Religious-themed records are often unusual simply because they were low budget, home-made creations.

and television, the most obscure and unknown examples from every cultural medium are being dredged up and given the attention that has so long been absent (usually in the form of some obsessive fan's webpage!) A simple search using an obscure name can turn up information that, as little as a decade ago, would have taken years of slow research to discover. Sometimes a quick check for information can turn up a whole new area of discovery. Recently I was online trying to find out more about the life of Ray 'Rae' Bourbon, obscure transvestite entertainer. Moments later, I discover *Dragstravaganza*, a website devoted entirely to records made by cross-dressing entertainers going back to the days of the Victrola! When your previous knowledge of the subject didn't go much beyond RuPaul and Divine, the discovery of the likes of Fist Goodbody and Effie Dropbottom can be quite an eye-opening experience, let me tell you! So while the digital age has all but spelled the end to the record album, at the same time the Internet has assured that even the most obscure relics will never be completely forgotten.

As some cliché-loving wit once said, 'I don't know about art, but I know what I like.' Likewise, I find it often difficult to explain what makes an album cover 'funny' or 'bad'... they just are! Many of these covers, of course, play off stereotypes. If vintage records were your only guide, you might think that Mexican citizens are issued sombreros and bandoleers at birth. Other records are simply reminders of a style of clothing or coiffure that most of us, especially those who wore it, would like to forget. Some are windows into a world that most know little about, like Christian ventriloquism or the transvestite club

7

scene. Whatever the case, my belief is that the 'worst' album covers are every bit as entertaining, enlightening and engaging as those on any art critic's 'best' covers list. And what could be more satisfying than rediscovering an artist that has otherwise been lost to history?

This book is dedicated to those who do what they do, not because it will make them a star or make them rich, or land their album cover in an art gallery, but simply because they *must* express themselves, whether on stage in front of thousands or alone in their basement.

Indeed, something else motivates those few who choose to make their work public... They really believe that their talent is too important to be kept secret. It's the same urge that, today, drives everyone from karaoke divas to 'pop idol' hopefuls. These artists demonstrate a desire to put their mark on history, to be recognized, to be able to say, 'I'm a recording artist.' And so, if these 20th century relics now bring us enjoyment in the new millennium, in a different way to that intended by their creators, does it really matter?

THE "WHERE ARE THEY NOW?" FILE

One of the most rewarding aspects of collecting these so-called 'bad' album covers is finding out more about the performers behind them.

The 'Where Are They Now?' file is my attempt not only to discover the current whereabouts of some of the characters responsible for these vinyl gems, but also simply to tell some entertaining stories from the lives of the artists. Although there's room for only a handful of tales here, some were just too good to leave out!

Ray Bourbon: The story of Ray Bourbon's life is something of a mystery, wrapped in an enigma, wrapped in an imported silk gown. Born on a Texas ranch circa 1892, he began his theatre career in London. By the early '20s he was on his way to Hollywood after winning a beauty contest from *Photoplay* magazine. The prize was a contract to appear in a Paramount movie! Unfortunately, studio brass was not amused to find that their contest winner was actually a man. They nevertheless found him work as a stand-in. He can be seen in the 1922 film *Blood and Sand* in a scene where his character dies in the arms of Rudolph Valentino. In the '30s, Bourbon developed his trademark risqué singing comedy act at 'Pansy Clubs' across America, and in the '40s he recorded dozens of 78-rpm records and opened his own swank club in Hollywood. By the '50s, the years were beginning to show, and he needed a gimmick to get back in the limelight. He needed to re-invent himself.

On May 23, 1956, *Variety* magazine broke the news, under the headline 'A Mexican Standoff': 'Ray Bourbon... has undergone a sex change operation in Mexico, and will return to show biz shortly as a femme.' Soon after, he released his best-known record, *Let Me Tell You About My Operation*. The event is now believed to be a hoax, but who's checking? His attempt to capitalize on the publicity was, however, not particularly successful. The aging Bourbon left LA and managed to eke out a living playing small theatres throughout the '60s, with an act involving his growing collection of dogs.

The beginning of the end came in 1968, when his ragged Cadillac and trailer broke down outside of Big Spring, Texas. Inside the trailer was Bourbon's beloved pet menagerie, estimated at 70 dogs, five cats and two skunks. While Ray went off to scare up some funds for a new car, he left the herd with local kennel owner A.D. Blount, who promptly sold the lot to a medical research firm. Bourbon was livid and hired some thugs from Kansas City to rough up Blount and find the dogs. Instead, the kennel owner ended up shot dead and the two thugs were convicted of murder. In February 1970, at 75 years of age,

LET ME TELL YOU ABOUT MY OPERATION

RAE BOURBON SPEAKING.....

UTC 7
HIGH INFIDELITY
A BROAD-RANGE RECORDING

LEFT: The story of Ray 'Rae' Bourbon is even more strange than his records!

Ray Bourbon was convicted on an accessory to murder charge and sentenced to 99 years in prison. He spent the next year writing his memoirs and petitioning celebrity friends for help but his Hollywood connections had no time for an old drag queen. He died in July 1971 in a small jail in the tiny city of Brownwood, Texas.

Fanny: It may be hard to believe, but Fanny's first album in 1970 was the first ever major-label album by an all-female rock band. Beatle George Harrison reportedly suggested the band's name, and early promotional efforts featured rear-shots of the band and slogans like 'Get Behind Fanny'. Their fifth and final album, *Rock and Roll Survivors*, was released in 1974, the band dissolving soon after. Although the band remains unknown even by most classic rock fans, others have ardently attempted to revive their memory. In a 1999 article in *Rolling Stone*, David Bowie said Fanny were 'one of the most important female bands in American rock... Revivify Fanny, and I will feel that my work is done.' Hopefully, Fanny's inclusion in this book will finally allow Bowie to relax.

The Good Twins: In 2003, Dwight and Dwayne Good attempted to break a world record by playing 102 concerts in 102 days. No word if they succeeded, but its a good bet that this devout duo didn't end up passed out in a Milwaukee drunk tank like the last band who tried it!

Johnny Hallyday: Hallyday is the biggest and pretty much only rock star in France. He shot to stardom in the early days of rock and roll as 'The French Elvis', playing French covers of American hits. In October 1966, in what would turn out to be one of those chance collisions of rock and roll superstars, Hallyday invited a then unknown American guitarist and his new band to open for a tour of his home nation. Thus The Jimi Hendrix Experience played its first-ever public performance opening up for a French cover band! As an enduring public figure, Hallyday has sold over 100 million records, starred in dozens of films and is a fixture on French TV, and yet he remains virtually unknown outside of the country. Oh – and here's an interesting tidbit – like fictional detective Hercule Poirot, Hallyday is not actually French, he's from Belgium.

Heino: German *überstar* Heino needs no introduction to readers from that country. By far the nation's most popular singer for over 30 years, his trademark blond moptop and square black sunglasses keep the *frauleins* swooning. In 1994, a group was formed to elect Heino president of Germany. Since I haven't heard anything, I assume he didn't win.

David Le Winter (The Pump Room): The legendary Pump Room in the Ambassador East Hotel has been a Chicago landmark since 1938. For 50 years, the swank eatery has seated everyone from Bette Davis and Humphry Bogart to Muhammad Ali

RIGHT: Even big-budget major label records can have strange covers, often unintentionally.

11

and Mick Jagger. In the '80s, a scruffy English rock drummer was refused entry because he did not meet the dress code. So distraught was he that he titled his next album after the incident. The underdressed Brit was none other than Phil Collins! Just think, without the Pump Room, there would be no *No Jacket Required*, no *One More Night*, no *Susudio*... The Pump Room, apparently with a new, hip vibe, is still open today, and, although there's still a dress code, Collins will be happy to know that jackets are no longer required.

Beverly Massegee: On November 22nd 1963, President John F. Kennedy was assassinated in Dealey Plaza in Dallas, Texas. One of the many enduring mysteries of the day is the identity of the so-called 'babushka lady', a be-scarved young woman, apparently holding a movie camera, who can be seen very close to the limousine at the moment of the shooting. The woman left the scene before being questioned or identified, and the mystery was born. Then in 1970, JFK researcher Gary Shaw met an aspiring ventriloquist named Beverly Oliver, who offhandedly claimed that she was 20 feet from Kennedy when he was shot. She had even filmed the incident, but the FBI had confiscated the footage. Shaw could hardly believe what he was hearing, but

after research became convinced that Beverly was telling the truth. In 1963, Beverly Oliver was a 17-year-old go-go dancer. She said she knew Ruby well. He had even introduced her to a man named Lee Oswald. Her film of the assassination, she claimed, was

LEFT: Does Erick the dummy have secret knowledge about the JFK asassination?

12

taken away days later by a man who identified himself as an FBI agent. 'I wasn't smart enough to ask for a receipt,' she explained in 1994.

Some time later, Ms. Oliver married a Baptist preacher and became a born-again Christian. As Beverly Massegee, she honed her ventriloquism skills and released the record we find here. She has also written a book of her Dealey Plaza experience, and has appeared on many television shows and documentaries as the 'babushka lady'. She was even a character in the Oliver Stone film, *JFK*. I don't know if Beverly was really there on that fateful day, but what I want to know is whether her dummy Erick knows more than he's letting on.

Jim Post: Jim is an interesting fellow. In addition to making 20 or so folk music records, he has written a book for children called *Frog in the Kitchen Sink*, produced several children's CDs, and is currently starring in a one-man Mark Twain tribute show of story and song. As a young man, he and his wife Cathy performed as a duo called Friend and Lover. They had a memorable hit with the hippie classic, *Reach Out of The Darkness* ('I think it's so groovy now, that people are finally getting together...'). Thus Jim Post was forever entered in the annals of one hit wonder history. None of this, however, explains the woodland shower album cover in this book. The wonders never cease!

There you have it, a few of the stories about the people behind the *Worst Album Covers in the World Volume 2*. I hope you enjoy the rest of the book. Maybe I'll see you checking out the racks in the record shops some time soon – just save some good ones for me!

Nick DiFonzo

artist **101 STRINGS**

title **The Soul of Poland**

The young starlet arrives in Hollywood with big dreams of a block-buster film role or modelling for a top fashion designer… An album cover photo shoot? This could be her big break! But after five minutes on this set, she's thinking, 'I've *got* to get a new agent…'

14

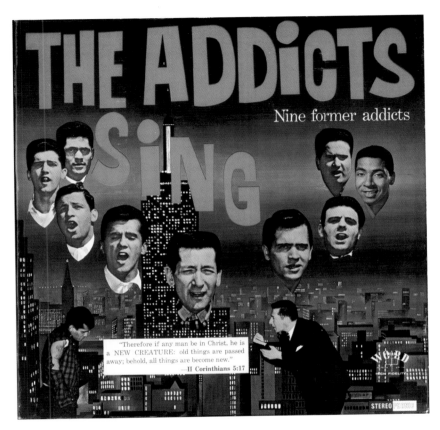

"Therefore if any man be in Christ, he is a NEW CREATURE: old things are passed away; behold, all things are become new."
—II Corinthians 5:17

artist   **THE ADDICTS**

title   **The Addicts Sing**

As anyone who lives downtown in a major city knows, the addicts *do* sing... usually at four in the morning outside your bedroom window! Thanks to this record, everyone can experience the fun!

artist **MIKE ADKINS**

title **Thank You For The Dove**

Ummmm… you're welcome? I'm not sure what Mike's plans are for this bird, but let's hope it doesn't involve pepper, chopped onions and a glass of dry white wine. I'm still waiting for his follow-up album, *I Just Ran Over A Squirrel*.

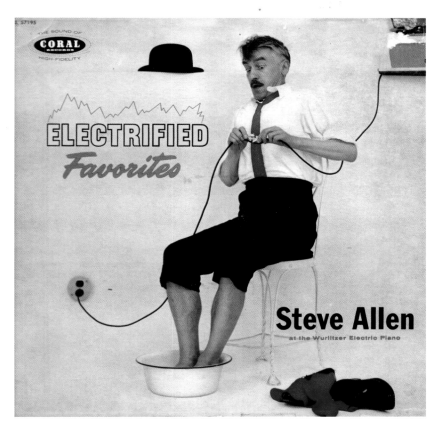

artist **STEVE ALLEN**

title **Electrified Favorites**

Here, a Dennis Farina lookalike shows us what *not* to do when listening to the record, which features one of those new-fangled 'electric' pianos. This album cover was in response to the tragic 'hi-fi foot bath' deaths of the '50s.

17

artist **CARROLL ATCHISON**

title **Come To The Chapel**

American Gothic meets *Phantasm*? This truly ghastly cover photo would be more appropriate for a horror movie poster. 'Yes, little one… Come to the Chapel of Doom! Muahahahahahaha!' Run, kids, while you still can!

18

THIS IS YOUR FUNERAL
If You Are a Christian

A Message by Dr. Dallas F. Billington

artist **DALLAS F. BILLINGTON**
title **This Is Your Funeral If You Are a Christian**

This is what you might call a 'feel-good' record, Baptist style. The front cover shows the happy scene you'll experience as a dead Christian. The back cover, entitled *This Is Your Funeral If You Die Unsaved*, shows the same casket with the lid closed.

19

LET ME TELL YOU ABOUT MY OPERATION

RAE BOURBON SPEAKING . . . . .

UTC 7

HIGH INFIDELITY
A BROAD RANGE RECORDING

artist **RAE BOURBON**
title **Let Me Tell You About My Operation**

Cross-dressing crooner Rae (*née* Ray) Bourbon shocked the entertainment community with his announcement of a Mexican sex change operation in 1956. Fine, Rae, you can tell me about your operation… Just keep the towel on, okay?

The Braillettes album cover — *Our Hearts Keep Singing*

His Smile
The Innkeeper
How Rich I Am
Tenderly He Calls
This Is My Prayer
He'll Never Let You Fall
All Day Long My Heart Keeps Singing
The First Thing I Do Every Morning
That's What He Did For Me
Will He Know Me?
Soon It Is Over

artist   **THE BRAILLETTES**

title   **Our Hearts Keep Singing**

Jackie, Maggie, and Kay were three young blind singers from California who brought their special vision to the 'spiritually blind'. This is truly a unique album cover that manages to be shocking, funny and kind of cute all at the same time!

17 YEARS IN PRISON
3 ½ YEARS IN SOLITARY CONFINEMENT
35 YEARS A DOPE ADDICT

but through

Nor-Vel
MUSIC CO.
presents

THE AMAZING GRACE OF GOD

A MINISTER OF THE GOSPEL

artist **JACK BROWN**

title **The Amazing Grace of God**

Here's a perfect example of a 'transformed man'. Jack Brown was a hopeless society drop-out, left with no skills after a long prison stint. But add a skinny tie and a microphone, and he's on the road, preaching the theory of 'Do as I say, not as I do!'

artist **CEPILLIN**
title **Un Dia con Mamá**

All clowns are scary, Mexican hippie clowns even more so. Add a Freudian fixation on his mother, and you have an awesomely bad album cover! Cepillin, which means 'little toothbrush', was a dentist before becoming host of a famous children's TV show.

artist   **CHICKEN Y SUS COMANDOS**

title   **A Mover "El Esqueleto"**

Where did they find these dancers? The hip-looking lady is believable, but the guy looks like a shoe salesman on crack. It's as if the Comandos dragged this couple off the street. Dance you fools! Dance as if Chicken himself compels you!

artist **CLAUDAR**

title **Présenté par Holiday Inn**

CLAUDe and ARmando, like many small-time lounge acts, made a
record to sell to hotel guests. One can only imagine the exciting
evening of dining, dancing, and hanky-panky that was surely had by
the original owner of this disc.

artist **THE CRAWFORD FAMILY**

title **Aboard Heaven's Choo-Choo**

Here, we see the happy Crawford Family all together. Mum and Dad seem blissfully unaware that in a few short years, Junior will likely be playing guitar in a Kiss cover band while Sis hitches across the country trying to 'find herself'.

JÁTÉK AZ ÉLET...

SLPM 37099
Stereo
(PROFIL

Dolly Roll

artist **DOLLY ROLL**
title ***Játék Az Élet...***

Records from 'foreign' nations are always a treat. You're never quite sure who these people are or what they're thinking. Are Hungary's Dolly Roll well-known in their own country? Who's pulling their strings? Does everyone in Hungary wear red vinyl?

B 1007

BELLAIRE RECORDS
PLAYABLE ON STEREO & MONO PHONOGRAPHS

MORE

OF

DON &

SEYMOUR

artist **DON & SEYMOUR**

title **More Of Don & Seymour**

Don & Seymour had a popular children's television show in Houston in the '60s. By this point in their careers, Seymour (pictured) was clearly taking control of the duo's artistic direction. It appears that Don wasn't even invited to the photoshoot for the cover.

artist **PEPPI ECKMAIR**

title **Der Jodel-Peppi vom Schliersee**

No holiday to Bavaria is complete without bringing home a yodelling record to remember the trip by. Luckily for the tourists, Peppi would come down from the mountains long enough to play a few gigs and sign a few records.

artist **THE ELECTRIC JUNKYARD**
title **The Electric Junkyard**

The year is 1969. In a small town of Woodstock, New York, many thousands gather for a festival that will become an icon for the decade. Neil Armstrong becomes the first human to set foot on the Moon. And this slacker sits in a bathtub, smoking a cigarette.

A comprehensive message delivered by Dr. Jerry Falwell, pastor, Thomas Road Baptist Church, Lynchburg, Va., which clearly answers man's most puzzling question.

The beautiful special music is provided by Doug Oldham and the Old-Time Gospel Hour choir.

Where are the Dead?

artist **DR. JERRY FALWELL**

title **Where are the Dead?**

The cover states that this record 'clearly answers man's most puzzling question.' For the fellows on the cover, that question may be something like, 'Where are the Dead? And how can we move them to build our new block of upscale condos?'

artist **FANNY**

title **Rock And Roll Survivors**

Fanny – the term has two different meanings in Britain and America, neither of which seems very appropriate for a girl glam rock band. This group may have been *Rock And Roll Survivors* but they washed up directly on to the beach of rock and roll obscurity.

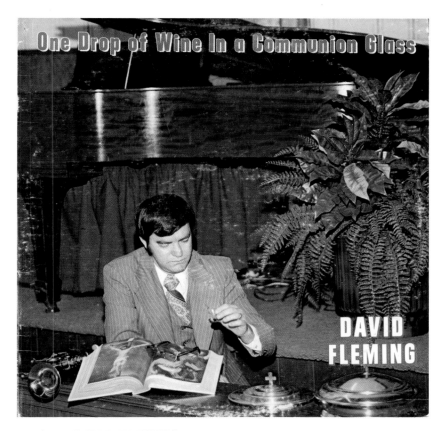

One Drop of Wine In a Communion Glass

artist **DAVID FLEMING**
title **One Drop of Wine In a Communion Glass**
This cover reminds me of a guy at a bar who can't believe his drink
is empty. You can tell he's had a few — he's holding his bible upside
down. To make this a country music album cover, you need only
change the title to *One Drop of Whiskey In a Shot Glass*.

artist **FURR**

title **Furr**

Every teen goes through an 'awkward phase', experimenting with new clothing, friends, and sexual identity. Rock and roll went through the same thing in the '70s. This band shows no small affinity for Kiss, the 'cool older kid' in the School of Rock.

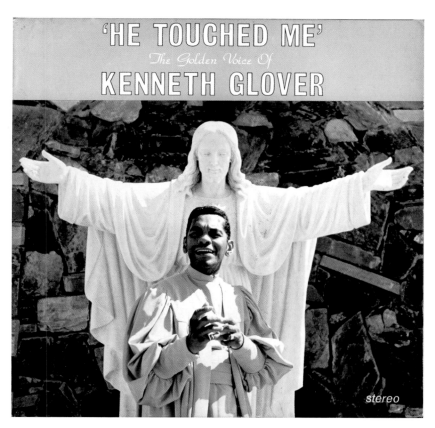

artist   **KENNETH GLOVER**

title   **'He Touched Me'**

Many religious-themed records talk about touching: *He Touched Me*; *Let Me Touch Him*; *I've Been Touched*. With all the touching going on, it must be tough to find time to pray!

35

The King Is Coming
and other favorites

featuring Rev. Frank Gonzales
and
"THE GOD SQUAD"

artist **REV. FRANK GONZALES AND "THE GOD SQUAD"**
title **The King Is Coming and other favorites**
You've heard of the Hell's Angels. You've seen She-Devils On Wheels. Now meet the God Squad! Yes, the Honda is revved up and ready to putter its way across the church car park to save your soul!

artist **THE GOOD TWINS**

title **Have Gospel Must Travel**

The Good Twins discover that singing the gospel doesn't always pay as well as one might hope. But surely, with their snappy dress and warm smile, a kindly Samaritan will stop and fill their tank!

artist **THE JAY GORDON CONCERT ORCHESTRA**
title **Music From Another World**
SEE!!! The movie poster models attacked by giant spirographs of light! HEAR!!! Second-rate renditions of moderately dull musical standards! THRILL!!! To the talents of the record company marketing men to make this record into a bestseller!

It's In My Heart

TTR-LP-1001

AS SUNG BY
Faber Grable

SIDE 1
It's In My Heart
The Stranger of Galilee
God Did a Wonderful Thing for Me
At the Altar
Seeking for Me
How Great Thou Art

SIDE 2
I'm Not Afraid Anymore
My Father Watches Over Me
Just a Closer Walk With Thee
Follow Me
What a Day That Will Be
Until Then

WITH PIANO, ORGAN, VIBRAHARP, CATHEDRAL CHIMES, HARP, GUITAR AND BASS VIOL

TEMPLETONE RECORDS

artist   **FABER GRABLE**
title   **It's In My Heart**

It's in his heart, and seemingly his digestive tract, as well. Take some laxatives and put the smile back on your face! In any case, this record is a good example of the home-made record, with the home-made cover and a made-up record label.

39

artist **"BALD" BILL HAGAN AND HIS TROCADERONS**
title **Music for a Strip Tease Party**
In the days before internet pornography, spicing up a love affair took some real effort. She had to buy curtains to make into lingerie. He had to roll out the hi-fi and put on this record. It would all be worth the effort, though, providing he was still around for side 2.

artist **DONNA HALL**

title **This is the Day**

This is the day… 10am: Joyce's Hair Salon… 11am: the thrift shop clearance rack… 12pm: collect leaves and twigs for props…1pm sharp: arrive at photo studio – 'autumn leaves' set… 1:15pm: make the album cover of a lifetime!

"LA PEUR"

PHILIPS

HALLYDAY

artist **JOHNNY HALLYDAY**

title **"La Peur"**

Johnny Hallyday is a well-known French singer who has been entertaining since the '60s. This record dates from the all-too-short *Mad
Max* era of rock and roll, a style which didn't go too far beyond this
record. Just walk away, Johnny, just walk away.

EFFECTIVE Soul Winning DEMONSTRATION

By Evangelist
CARL HATCH

DEMONSTRATION

artist **CARL HATCH**
title **Effective Soul Winning Demonstration**

We've seen instructional records and preacher records, so it's a real treat to find an instructional preacher record. If you're the type of guy who *wants* to win souls, but just can't get the whole 'knocking on doors' and 'reading from the bible' stuff down, this record is for you!

43

artist **HEINO**

title **Deutsche Weihnacht ...und festliche Lieder**

Heino… the most popular German singer ever, and one of the most famous celebrities in the country. This Christmas album is but one of a seemingly endless number of his records, all featuring his trademark blond hair and dark glasses. *O Tannenbaum*, indeed.

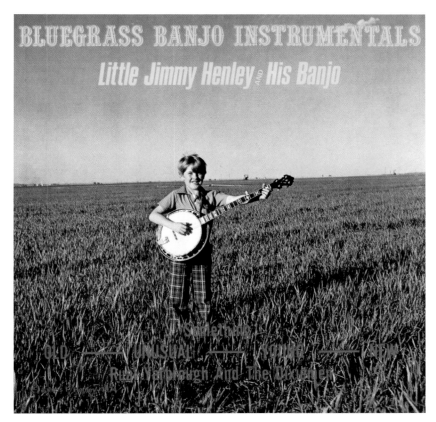

artist **LITTLE JIMMY HENLEY AND HIS BANJO**

title **Bluegrass Banjo Instrumentals**

Child musicians are a perennial source of fascination in Western culture. From Mozart to Michael Jackson, some of our greatest artists began their careers as children, usually pushed in no small measure by well-meaning parents.

artist **HIGH NOON**

title **Bendin' Rules & Breakin' Hearts**

In the mid-'80s, hairstyles and country music reached all-time low points. Both can be seen in the record by this Minnesota-based bunch, who somewhat unwisely have committed their stylistic confusion to the realm of album cover history, forever.

artist **THE HOT CZECHS**

title ***Goin' Bankin'***

The small-town band often ends up in odd arrangements with the small-town business. When The Hot Czechs needed some cash for their used Winnebago and blue tuxedos, the local bank was the perfect match!

HOT LINE TO HEAVEN

JERRY IRBY

STEREO LP-92875

artist   **JERRY IRBY**

title   **Hot Line To Heaven**

Jerry Irby was a country and rock-a-billy star for some 30 years before, like so many other such artists, he 'saw the light' and turned his attention to religious-themed recordings. Unlike many others, however, he seems to have kept his sense of humour and fun intact.

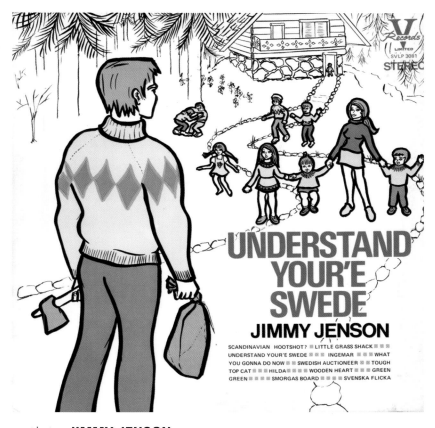

artist **JIMMY JENSON**

title **Understand Your'e Swede**

OK, I can see why Jimmy has so many kids – his wife is certainly a hottie. But the tranquil scene of Nordic bliss is somewhat tempered by the strange objects Mr. Jenson is carrying. What's he going to do with that hatchet? And what on earth is in that sack?

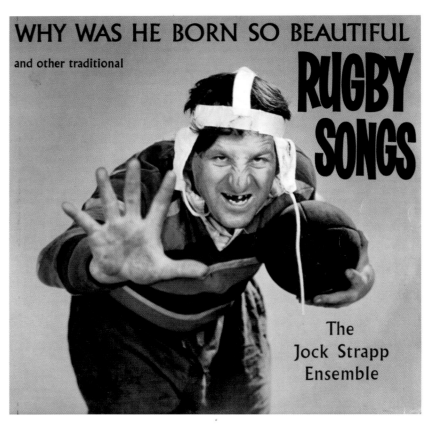

artist **THE JOCK STRAPP ENSEMBLE**

title **Why Was He Born So Beautiful...**

Few things go together better than the game of rugby and drunken public house caterwauling. Such tunes as *Dinah, Show Us Your Legs* and *The Balls of O'Leary* are sure to be familiar to all players of the game, as well as those unfortunate enough to live nearby.

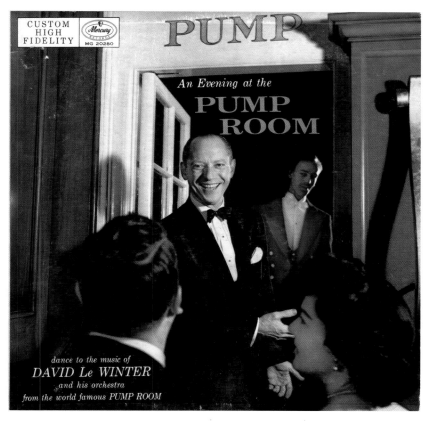

artist **DAVID LE WINTER**

title ***An Evening at the Pump Room***

Honey, where are you taking me this time? The Pump Room? Why is it so dark inside? Is this another one of those 'special clubs' that you're always visiting late at night? Why, that boy in red seems to know you… What exactly do they serve here, anyway?

artist **LOS FABULOSOS CUATRO**

title **Rancheras**

Arriba! This jaunty bunch from 'south of the border' is trying very hard to be the Mexican 'Fab Four'. This cover is like *A Hard Day's Night*, but with shotguns and sombreros instead of guitars and moptops.

A VOX STEREOPHONIC RECORDING STPL 515.080

LOS INDIOS TABA-JARAS

POPULAR AND
FOLK SONGS
OF LATIN
AMERICA

" *Chants et Danses*
du folklore
d'Amérique Latine "

artist   **LOS INDIOS TABA-JARAS**
title   **Popular And Folk Songs Of Latin America**

While some records use ethnic stereotypes, others resort to pure
fantasy. Who are these guys supposed to be – bellydancing pirate
clowns? It's as if they raided a costume shop and just took the
weirdest things they could find!

RICHARD MALTBY and his orchestra play...

MUSIC TO RECLINE BY in a BERKLINE chair

BERKLINE CHAIRS COVERED IN
Algiers PLYHIDE

SPECIALLY PRESSED by
RCA
CUSTOM RECORDS

artist **RICHARD MALTBY AND HIS ORCHESTRA**
title **Music to Recline by in a Berkline Chair**

This record attempts to cash in on the hi-fi craze by making the 'Plyhide' recliner chair a must-have stereo accessory. Just don't move around much… the annoying squeaks of the fake leather will drown out the music!

artist **BUZZ MARTIN**
title **Where There Walks a Logger There Walks a Man**
Before being forever tainted by the Monty Python 'lumberjack' skit, the profession of the logger was an honorable, manly one. Buzz was the best known of the 'logger poets', with songs such as *Whistle Punk Pete* and *Sick of Settin' Chokers*.

artist **BEVERLY AND ERICK MASSEGEE**

title **Amen!**

There is something so phenomenally creepy about this record that it's hard to pinpoint. Maybe its Erick's crumbling eyelids. Maybe it's that his hair looks more real than Beverly's. Maybe I can't stand to think about it anymore!

artist **THE McDONALD SISTERS**

title **"I've Got Confidence"**

When people see my record collection, they'll often ask, 'Are these covers for real?' My answer is this record. Could anyone make this up? What better way to make a couple of awkward teens (named Edwina and Jorene) even *more* self-conscious?

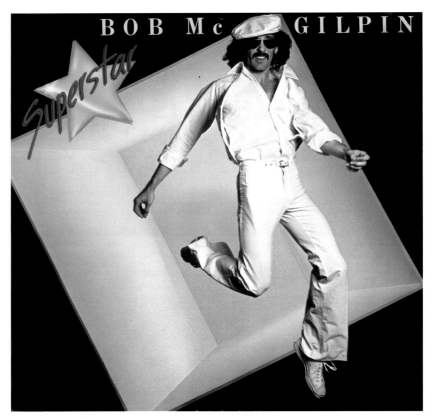

artist **BOB McGILPIN**

title ***Superstar***

This guy looks like he's running a marathon on tiptoe. Or maybe he's escaping from a mob of fans… He is a 'superstar' after all. Or maybe I'm just sad that a man can no longer go out in public in white bell-bottoms and a beret without being called 'light in the loafers'.

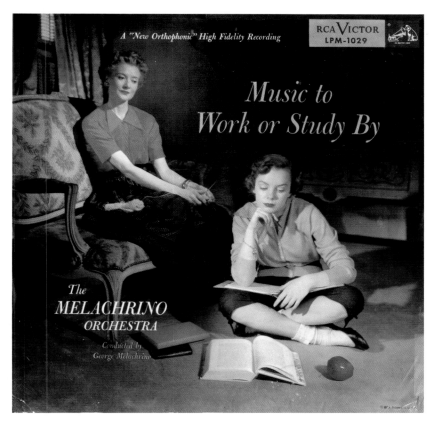

A "New Orthophonic" High Fidelity Recording

RCA VICTOR
LPM-1029

Music to Work or Study By

The MELACHRINO ORCHESTRA
Conducted by George Melachrino

artist **THE MELACHRINO ORCHESTRA**

title **Music to Work or Study By**

This cover needs a modern update. I see daughter at her laptop, chattering away on her mobile phone while munching away at a low-GI crisps. Meanwhile, mother complains about how the living room just doesn't look like the one on the interior design programme.

THE ETHEL MERMAN DISCO ALBUM

artist **ETHEL MERMAN**

title **The Ethel Merman Disco Album**

From grande dame of Broadway to old diva of disco, Ethel could
conquer anything. Except Ernest Borgnine. Yes, Ethel married
'Marty' in 1964, only to be divorced 32 days later. Maybe that's him
with the cowboy hat, warning us of a country music album to come.

FULL DIMENSIONAL STEREO

THEY SAID IT COULDN'T BE DONE!

BUT THEY DIDN'T RECKON WITH THE MIGHTY ACCORDION BAND

artist **THE MIGHTY ACCORDION BAND**

title **They Said It Couldn't Be Done!**

When you're faced with trying to sell something patently uncool (in this case, a band of 20 accordions) to a young, hip audience, only one solution makes sense: apes! From gorilla to gibbon, nothing says 'buy me' like our simian friends!

61

MRS. MILLS
KNEES-UP PARTY

Down at the old Bull and Bush
The man on the flying trapeze   Knees up Mother Brown
For me and my gal   Don't dilly dally on the way
Waiting for the Robert E. Lee   Y Viva Espana
Can Can   Bye bye Blackbird
Lambeth Walk
Yellow Submarine
AND MANY MORE

artist   **MRS. MILLS**
title   **Knees-Up Party**

A party just isn't a party without a singing grandmother. This cover shows why they don't have pubs in retirement homes. You never know what kind of crazy things they'll do! I must say, pensioners in the US don't seem to have this much fun.

artist **MONTEUX VIENNA PHILHARMONIC**

title ***Symphonie Fantastique***

In the '50s, designers of classical music album covers had to compete with the new wave of pin-up girl exotica. The sellers of this record tried a new technique, that might have been subtitled, 'Buy this record or we hang this model!'

ON THE ROAD AGAIN

David Osborne

artist **DAVID OSBORNE**
title **On the Road Again**

David Osborne, before becoming known as the 'Pianist to the Presidents', was apparently the 'Pianist to his Car'. Sure, everyone's proud of their first ride, but is it necessary to put it on your album cover? Now I see where all the rappers got it from!

artist   **REG OWEN AND HIS ORCHESTRA**
title   **Coffee Break**

The sleeve notes say, 'The coffee break is as much a part of life today as peanut brittle, carbon paper, filter-tipped cigarettes, and liquid detergents.' I couldn't have said it better myself!

STEREO 2877

Dance Into Your Sultan's Heart

Belly Dance with Özel

The Newest fun way to exercise...and excite! Includes easy-to-follow, illustrated instruction booklet.

ELEC RECORDS

artist **OZEL**

title **Dance Into Your Sultan's Heart**

An authentic bellydance from a pro like Ozel can be a beautiful and sensual experience. Actually, I'm just guessing about that. I would also guess that learning the sultry art of bellydancing from an album is sure to lead to a bedroom disaster of Biblical proportions!

From Our House to Yours

SINGING: faith, home & country

artist **THE RON PATTY FAMILY**

title **From Our House to Yours**

Apparently, the highways of America were once filled with singing families criss-crossing the country. Imagine the excitement of an impromptu caravan park show if you happened to be staying at the campsite next to theirs! Sounds like a good reason to stay at home.

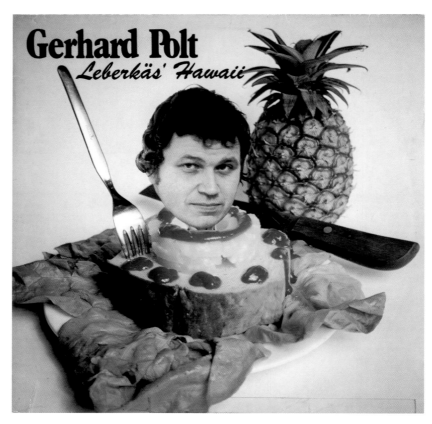

artist **GERHARD POLT**

title **Leberkäs' Hawaii**

'Foreign' album covers are always the most inexplicable. Sure, I could translate the German song titles to give me a clue why Herr Polt chose to perch his head atop a lovely ham and pineapple dish, but where's the fun in that?

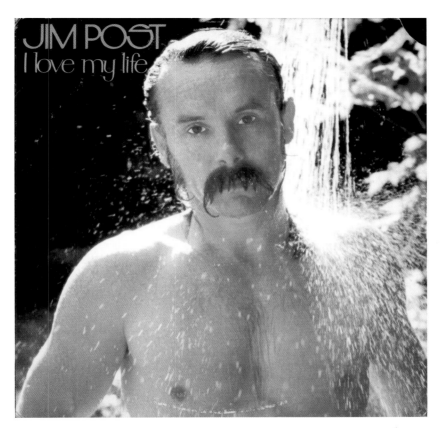

artist **JIM POST**

title **I love my life**

Showering in the forest is strange enough. Choosing this event for your album cover is beyond my abilities to explain. Let's just say that if you ever run across this scene in real life, its a good bet that you're at the wrong beach!

69

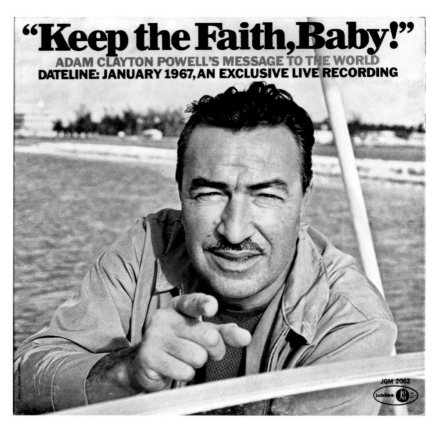

artist   **ADAM CLAYTON POWELL**

title   **"Keep the Faith, Baby!"**

From the Telly Savalas school of vinyl comes this relic by the US Congressman from Harlem, NY. Although he was from the big city, he seems to have enjoyed spending time on his yacht! I'm sure he's just sailing down to Washington to get some work done.

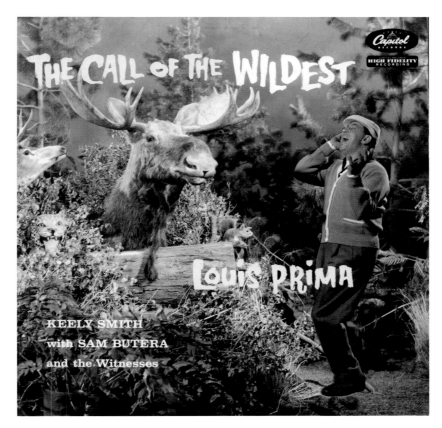

artist **LOUIS PRIMA**

title **The Call of the Wildest**

Big budget does not always mean big ideas. These designers obviously raided some executive's office for hunting trophies – let's hope they put them back before he returned from safari. So, if Louis Prima scats in the forest, does it make a sound?

artist **THE REBELS QUARTET**

title **What Then?**

The obsession with atomic Armageddon in the '50s was evident in books, movies, television, and music. Apparently, when the problems of the world have you feeling down, there's nothing like some good old-fashioned post-apocalyptic gospel singing to pep you up!

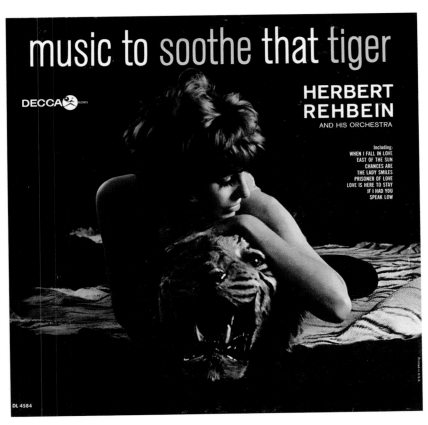

music to soothe that tiger

HERBERT REHBEIN
AND HIS ORCHESTRA

Including:
WHEN I FALL IN LOVE
EAST OF THE SUN
CHANCES ARE
THE LADY SMILES
PRISONER OF LOVE
LOVE IS HERE TO STAY
IF I HAD YOU
SPEAK LOW

DECCA RECORDS

DL 4584

artist   **HERBERT REHBEIN AND HIS ORCHESTRA**
title   **Music To Soothe That Tiger**

It must have been nice, back in the days before the meddling 'conservationists' had us all feeling guilty about stepping on an ant. I long for the days when a man could gun down an endangered species, gut it, toss it on the floor, and see the ladies come running!

73

STEREO (ALSO PLAYABLE MONO)

CALLS OF THE BUSHVELD

Recordings by: DICK REUCASSEL AND TONY POOLEY Script and narration by: HUGH ROUSE

Golden Disc Award

artist **DICK REUCASSEL AND TONY POOLEY**

title **Calls of the Bushveld**

As this close-up cover shot shows, wildlife photography has come a long way. *Yaawwn!* Oh, I mean *Roaaar!* The photographer must have really put his life on the line to capture this pair of hungry, man-eating beasts.

"*How Much More*"

artist **STEVE REYNOLDS**

title **"How Much More"**

Since the dawn of civilization, it has been a dream of mankind to harness nature and bend the animal world to his will. On this cover, Steve lives the dream, as he cavorts with his collection of stuffed forest animals. *How Much More?* Well, a bear would be nice…

75

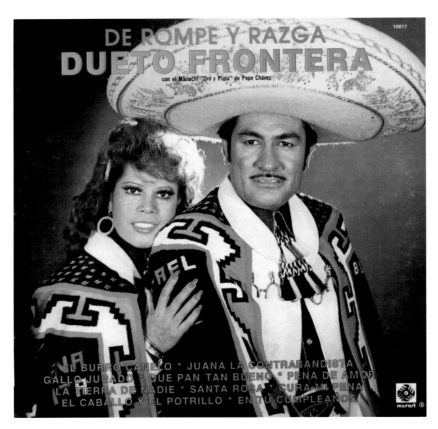

artist **DE ROMPE Y RAZGA**

title **Dueto Frontera**

These two look like they just spent the day living it up at a Tijuana flea market! You know your hat is big when it smashes into the hair of the person standing next to you. Perhaps that's why the oversized sombrero never caught on around the world…

76

artist **SEBASTIAN**

title **Sebastian Speaks!**

What a great idea! A recording of a vicious dog, played on your turntable to scare off burglars! So, when you leave for the day, this record would protect your house... Well, for about 20 minutes, anyway, unless you can teach your cat to flip the record over.

artist   **THE SEGO BROTHERS & NAOMI**
title   **Jesus is a Soul Man**

Here's one where the cover photo makes all the difference. Given the title, you might think you're buying an album of James Brown-style funky grooves. The cover will quickly dispel that idea. Let's just say, the Sego Brothers have a brand new bag.

artist **KATHY SHADOWS**

title **A Stroll Through The Emerald Isle**

There's nothing like the lilting melodies of a beautiful Irish lass to bring back memories of the old country. From foggy moor to craggy castle, the authentic sounds of Eire are here to enjoy, courtesy of Ms. Shadows – a lounge singer from Texas!

79

artist **SHARLENE SHARP**

title **Rare and Well Done**

Sonny Look was a Houston restaurateur whose 'Sir-Loin' club featured jousting knights on horseback. Here, he's pictured with his latest acquisition, singer Sharlene Sharp. I know it's Texas and all, but is drunk horse-riding legal?

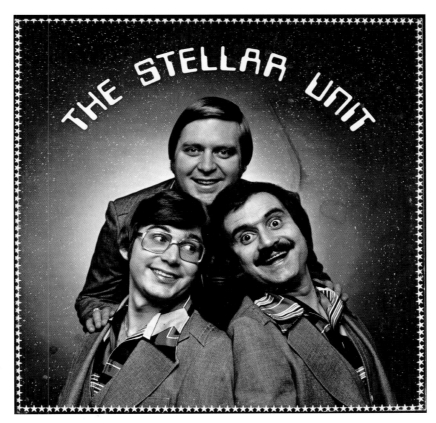

artist   **THE STELLAR UNIT**
title   **The Stellar Unit**

Nerd alert! Nerd alert! Man, these guys have it all. The polyester print shirts, square glasses, even the retro-futuristic computer font. I don't know much about these chaps, but I'll bet at least one of them can fix my computer.

artist **YMA SUMAC**

title ***Fuego del Ande***

Yma Sumac was a Peruvian chanteuse who could not only converse with the birds but also send them fleeing into the trees with their ears ringing. Rumours abounded that she was actually a Brooklyn house-wife named Amy Camus, but she *was* actually from South America!

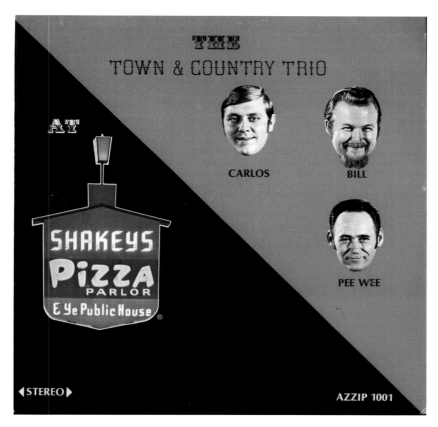

artist **THE TOWN & COUNTRY TRIO**
title **At Shakeys Pizza Parlor & Ye Public House**
You know you've made it big when your band releases its debut album. And, when there's a tie-in with a famous pizza buffet, you know you're getting a lot of free pizza into the bargain. You may recognize Carlos from page 81 – he's in The Stellar Unit, too!

83

artist **THE TWIN CITY SINGERS**

title **A Touch of Variety**

I see why they wear matching suits. Otherwise you wouldn't even think these guys were from the same planet, let alone in the same group. Oh, and Grandma? Better check on those old curtains you had in the closet. I think you'll find them missing.

artist **DR. JACK VAN IMPE**

title **Hell Without Hell, Is It The Grave?**

In his lifelong crusade to scare the wits out of his followers, Dr. Van Impe always paints a harrowing picture of the underworld. Here, he seems to have enlisted the help of the 'Nauga', the mascot for a popular brand of '60s fabric. I don't get it either.

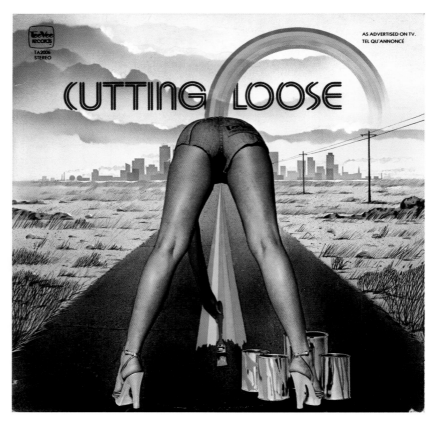

artist **VARIOUS ARTISTS**

title ***Cutting Loose***

Nothing says 'sexy' like a woman's crotch squirting rainbows on the asphalt. At least that's what these cover designers thought! Nothing here makes any sense. Why is she painting the road? Why is she in the desert? And where, pray tell, is the pot of gold?

BANDA SONORA ORIGINAL DE LA PELÍCULA

LAS AVENTURAS DE ENRIQUE y Ana

ESTEREO
304-0078

artist   **VARIOUS ARTISTS**

title   **Las Aventuras De Enrique y Ana**

With all the cable television channels around these days, how come they never show the good stuff? This soundtrack from the 1981 Spanish film serves only to whet my appetite to see it.

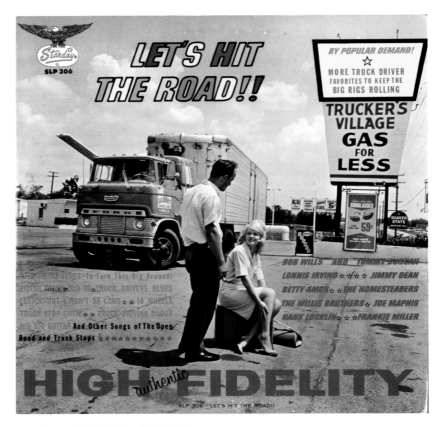

artist **VARIOUS ARTISTS**

title **Let's Hit The Road!!**

Hey, honey, where you goin'? Well, what d'ya know, I'm headed that way. If you're looking for smooth drivin', I'm your man. I've got 18 wheels and a diesel that won't quit. So what do you say, honey? Let's hit the road!

SOUL FEELIN'

Wilson Pickett
Lloyd Price
Lou Rawls
The Isley Brothers
Little Richard

The Shirelles
Nancy Wilson
King Curtis
Jerry Butler
Cannonball Adderley

artist **VARIOUS ARTISTS**

title **Soul Feelin'**

That soul feelin'… It's all about the hair! Soul music was big in the '70s, but the hair was bigger. Shape was also important: a perfectly round hair-do symbolized harmony, peace, and quality hair products. Just don't get that lollipop too close!

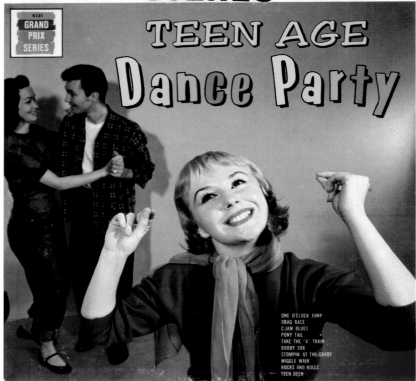

FULL FREQUENCY **STEREO** FULL FREQUENCY

K131
GRAND
PRIX
SERIES

TEEN AGE
Dance Party

ONE O'CLOCK JUMP
DRAG RACE
C-JAM BLUES
PONY TAIL
TAKE THE "A" TRAIN
BOBBY SOX
STOMPIN AT THE SAVOY
WIGGLE WALK
ROCKS AND ROLLS
TEEN DEEN

artist **VARIOUS ARTISTS**
title **Teen Age Dance Party**

Can you believe it? Bobby actually came to *my* party! I know he's
dancing with Suzie now, but I'll change that! Let me just put on a
new record. Maybe if I stand over here alone, he'll ask me to dance.
Bobby? Suzie? Where did you go?

90

artist **FEDERICO VELLANOWETH**

title ***Gimnasia En Su Hogar***

It's no stretch to say that the exercise craze is a worldwide phenom-
enon. As this record shows, even if you can't afford membership at
a fancy health club, you can turn your lounge into a gym with the
simple addition of some Astroturf and a beauty in a leotard.

artist **FERNANDITO VILLALONA**
title *Ayer y Hoy*

Subtlety is not a trait embraced by album cover designers in Mexico. It's obvious that this cover is meant to do only one thing: sell bananas. Yes, the fruit lobby is strong in the music industry, and no promotional opportunity is to be passed up. Peel away!

92

artist **THE GUY WARREN SOUNDS**

title **Themes for African Drums**

In the suburbs of post-war America, middle-class neighbourhoods began to get more colourful. Record companies responded quickly. This flaming native tells us more about the prejudices of its target audience than it does about the music!

FURTHER INFORMATION

Artists' Websites

Steve Allen:
www.steveallenonline.com

Honeytree:
www.honeytree.org

Dolly Roll:
www.dollyroll.hu

The Pump Room:
www.pumproom.com

The Good Twins:
www.thegoodtwins.com

Beverly Massegee:
www.massegee.org

Johnny Hallyday:
johnnyhallyday.artistes.universalmusic.fr

Jim Post:
www.jimpost.com

High Noon:
www.highnoon.to

Other Websites

The Author's Website:
www.bizarrerecords.com

Belly Dance Records:
www.radiobastet.com

All Music Guide:
www.allmusic.com/

Whistling Records:
www.whistlingrecords.com

Dragstravaganza:
www.blakstone.com/Dragstravaganza
%20Site

PICTURE ACKNOWLEDGEMENTS

All the album covers featured are from the author's collection.

The publishers would like to thank all artists and recording companies who agreed to be included in the book. Every effort was made to contact the parties concerned with the copyright of these album covers.

Gerhard Polt, *Leberkäs' Hawaii* appears courtesy Jupiter-Records, Germany. Jim Post, *I Love My Life* used by permission of Stephen Powers and Mountain Railroad Records.

AUTHOR ACKNOWLEDGEMENTS

Thanks to Alison Bale, John Spath, Matt Murillo, Chris DiFonzo and all the other people who have found records for me over the years. Thanks to the people of Rudyard's Pub, who have proven that this book is a lot funnier after a few drinks.

Most of all thanks to the people of Houston, Texas, and their horrible taste in records, without which this book would not have been possible.

First published in 2005 by New Holland Publishers (UK) Ltd
London • Cape Town • Sydney • Auckland

www.newhollandpublishers.com

Garfield House, 86–88 Edgware Road, London W2 2EA, United Kingdom

80 McKenzie Street, Cape Town 8001, South Africa

14 Aquatic Drive, Frenchs Forest, NSW 2086, Australia

218 Lake Road, Northcote, Auckland, New Zealand

10 9 8 7 6 5 4 3 2 1

ISBN 1 84537 244 1

Publishing Manager: Jo Hemmings
Editor: Gareth Jones
Cover Design and Design: Adam Morris
Production: Joan Woodroffe

Reproduction by Modern Age Repro House Ltd, Hong Kong
Printed and bound by Craft Print International Pte Ltd, Singapore

Publisher's Note:
Every effort has been made to contact the parties concerned with the copyright of these album
covers. Any further information pertaining to copyright will be included in future editions.